ROYAL COURT

The Royal Court Theatre presents

THE HERETIC
by **RICHARD BEAN**

First performance at The Royal Court Jerwood Theatre Downstairs, Sloane Square,
London on Friday 4 February 2011.

THE HERETIC

by Richard Bean

in order of appearance
Dr Diane Cassell **Juliet Stevenson**
Phoebe **Lydia Wilson**
Ben Shotter **Johnny Flynn**
Geoff Tordoff **Adrian Hood**
Professor Kevin Maloney **James Fleet**
Catherine Tickell **Leah Whitaker**

Director **Jeremy Herrin**
Designer **Peter McKintosh**
Lighting Designer **Paul Pyant**
Sound Designer **Emma Laxton**
Casting Director **Julia Horan**
Assistant Director **Sophie Austin**
Production Manager **Paul Handley**
Stage Manager **Ben Delfont**
Deputy Stage Manager **Tilly Stokes**
Assistant Stage Manager **Laura Draper**
Stage Management Placement **Louis Carver**
Costume Supervisor **Iona Kenrick**
Fight Director **Kevin McCurdy**
Set built by **Scena**
Painted by **Charlotte Gainey**

The Royal Court Theatre and Stage Management wish to thank the following for their help on this production: Bryn Austin, Department of Earth Sciences at UCL, Dorset Cereal Company, Robin Fisher, Franke UK Ltd, Grove Organic Fruit Company, Ruth Murfitt, Nature Magazine, Jeremy Paxman and the BBC Newsnight team, Rangemaster, Rose Skiera, Keith Stephens at The Royal Holloway University, Chris and Sylvia Stokes, Tyrells Hand Cooked Potato Chips and Robbie Wilmot.

The Heretic by Richard Bean was originally commissioned by Sonia Friedman Productions.

THE COMPANY

RICHARD BEAN (Writer)

FOR THE ROYAL COURT: Harvest, Honeymoon Suite (& ETC), Under the Whaleback, Toast.

OTHER THEATRE INCLUDES: The Big Fellah (Out of Joint/tour); House of Games, The Hypochondriac (adaptations, Almeida); Pub Quiz is Life, Up on Roof (Hull Truck); On the Side of the Angels (The Great Game, Tricycle); England People Very Nice, The Mentalists, Wabenzi (National); The English Game (Headlong/tour); In the Club (Hampstead/tour); The God Botherers (Bush); Smack Family Robinson (Live, Newcastle); Mr England (Sheffield Crucible).

RADIO INCLUDES: Of Rats and Men, Yesterday, Unsinkable, Robin Hood's Revenge.

AWARDS INCLUDE: 2005 Critics' Circle Best Play Award for Harvest, 2004 Pearson Play of the Year Award for Honeymoon Suite, 2002 George Devine Award for Under the Whaleback.

SOPHIE AUSTIN (Assistant Director)

AS DIRECTOR THEATRE INCLUDES: Adventures in Wonderland, Hothouse, Three Sisters, Twelfth Night, Romeo and Juliet (Site Specific, Teatro Vivo); The Colorado Session (Manchester 24:7 Festival).

AS ASSISTANT DIRECTOR: As You Like It (Curve, Leicester); Shrieks of Laughter (Soho); The Water Engine (Theatre 503/Young Vic); Chaos (The Door); Dead Hands (Riverside Studios); The Life of Galileo (BAC).

Sophie is Artistic Director of Teatro Vivo and Creative Associate at Dash Arts.

JAMES FLEET (Professor Kevin Maloney)

THEATRE INCLUDES: Twelfth Night, The Churchill Play, The Taming of the Shrew, Hyde Park, The Jew of Malta, Waste, The Dillen, Volpone, A New Way to Pay Old Debts, The Time of Your Life, Peter Pan, Henry IV Parts I & II, Money, The Witch of Edmonton, A Midsummer Night's Dream (RSC); The Observer, Berenice (National); In the Club (Hampstead/tour); Cloud Nine (Almeida); Habeas Corpus (Bath Theatre Royal/tour); Mary Stuart (Donmar); Three Sisters, Art (West End); The Late Middle Classes (UK tour); Neville's Island (Nottingham Playhouse); Just Between Ourselves, As You Like It (Old Vic); The Government Inspector (Greenwich Playhouse); The Crimson Island, Winterset, An Orange for Baby, Up in the Hide (Gate).

TELEVISION INCLUDES: Being Human, Coronation Street, Micro Men, Skins, Hotel Babylon, Little Dorrit, Harley Street, Legit, Midsomer Murders, Sea of Souls, Monarch of the Glen, Murder in Suburbia, Family Business, Promoted to Glory, Young Arthur, Fields of Gold, Dick Whittington, Brotherly Love, Chambers, Spark, Underworld, Dance to the Music of Time, Cows, Crossing the Floor, Harry Enfield and Chums, Moll Flanders, Lord of Misrule, The Vicar of Dibley, Milner, Cracker, Murder Most Horrid, Running Late, Head Hunters, A Year in Provence, The Bill, Boon, The Common Pursuit, They Never Slept, Grange Hill, Omega Factor.

FILM INCLUDES: The Decoy Bride, Tristram Shandy: A Cock and Bull Story, Lady Godiva: Back in the Saddle, The Phantom of the Opera, Blackball, South from Granada, Two Men Went to War, Charlotte Gray, Kevin and Perry, Milk, Frenchman's Creek, Remember Me, Eskimo Day, Butterfly Effect, The Grotesque, Sense and Sensibility, Three Steps to Heaven, Four Weddings and a Funeral, Exchange of Fire, Femme Fatale, Blue Black Permanent, An Electric Moon, Defence of the Realm.

JOHNNY FLYNN (Ben Shotter)

THEATRE INCLUDES: Twelfth Night, The Taming of the Shrew (Propeller).

TELEVISION INCLUDES: Kingdom, Holby City, Murder in Suburbia.

FILM INCLUDES: Lotus Eaters, Crusade in Jeans.

JEREMY HERRIN (Director)

FOR THE ROYAL COURT: Kin, Spur of the Moment, Off the Endz, The Priory, Tusk Tusk, The Vertical Hour, That Face (& Duke of York's).

OTHER THEATRE INCLUDES: Marble (Abbey, Dublin); The Family Reunion (Donmar); Blackbird (Market Theatre, Johannesburg); Statement of Regret (National); Sudden Collapses in Public Places, The Boy on the Swing, Gathered Dust and Dead Skin, The Lovers, Our Kind of Fun, Toast, Dirty Nets, Smack Family Robinson, Attachments, From the Underworld, The Last Post, Personal Belongings, ne1, Knives in Hens (Live Theatre).

FOR THE ROYAL COURT, AS ASSISTANT DIRECTOR: My Night with Reg, Babies, Thyestes, The Kitchen.

FILM & TELEVISION INCLUDES: Linked, Dead Terry, Warmth, Cold Calling.

Jeremy is Deputy Artistic Director of the Royal Court.

ADRIAN HOOD (Geoff Tordoff)

FOR THE ROYAL COURT: Harvest.

OTHER THEATRE INCLUDES: Pub Quiz is Life, Perfect Pitch, Our House, Billy Liar, Stand, A Weekend in England (Hull Truck); The Rise and Fall of Little Voice (National/West End); Up 'n' Under (Liverpool Playhouse/West End/tour); Fly Me to the Moon (Stephen Joseph Theatre, Scarborough); The Jungle Book (Cumbernauld Theatre); Stirrings in Sheffield (Sheffield Crucible).

TELEVISION INCLUDES: Zen, Kingdom, The Invisibles, The Last Detective, Johnny Shakespeare, Not Going Out, Oddsquad, Feel the Force, Micawber, dinnerladies, The Preston Front, Thunder Road, Buried, The Bill, The Royal, Sweet Medicine, Stan the Man, Heartbeat, Victoria Wood with all the Trimmings, Where The Heart Is, Witness Against Hitler, Harry, My Kingdom for a Horse, Small Zones, Surviving Disaster, Chernobyl, Hibbert and Long.

FILM INCLUDES: Magicians, Brassed Off, Up 'n' Under.

EMMA LAXTON (Sound Designer)

FOR THE ROYAL COURT: Off the Endz, Tusk Tusk, Faces in the Crowd, That Face (& Duke of York's), Gone Too Far!, Catch, Scenes From The Back Of Beyond, Woman and Scarecrow, The World's Biggest Diamond, Incomplete & Random Acts of Kindness, My Name is Rachel Corrie (& Playhouse/Minetta Lane, New York/Galway Festival/Edinburgh Festival), Bone, The Weather, Bear Hug, Terrorism, Food Chain.

OTHER THEATRE INCLUDES: Men Should Weep (Lyttleton, National Theatre); Charged 1 & 2 (Clean Break at Soho Theatre); My Romantic History (Bush/Sheffield Theatres), Like A Fishbone, The Whisky Taster, If There Is I Haven't Found It Yet, 2nd May 1997, Apologia, The Contingency Plan, Wrecks, Broken Space Season, 2000 Feet Away, Tinderbox (Bush); Travels With My Aunt (Northampton Royal); Sisters (Sheffield Theatres); Timing (King's Head), Ghosts (ATC at Arcola); Treasure Island (Theatre Royal Haymarket); A Christmas Carol (Chichester Festival Theatre); Pornography (Birmingham Rep/Traverse); Shoot/Get Treasure/Repeat (National); Europe (Dundee Rep/Barbican Pit); Other Hands (Soho); The Unthinkable (Sheffield Crucible); My Dad's a Birdman (Young Vic); The Gods Are Not To Blame (Arcola).
Emma is an Associate Artist at the Bush Theatre and the Associate Sound Designer of War Horse.

PETER McKINTOSH (Designer)

TELEVISION INCLUDES: The 39 Steps (New York/Boston/Australia/Korea/China/ Russia/Japan/Israel/Italy/UK tours); Love Story, Shirley Valentine and Educating Rita, Prick Up Your Ears, Entertaining Mr Sloane, Fiddler on the Roof, The Dumb Waiter, Summer and Smoke, Donkeys' Years, The Home Place, The Birthday Party, Ying Tong, A Woman of No Importance and Boston Marriage (West End); King John, Brand, The Merry Wives of Windsor, Pericles, Alice in Wonderland (RSC); Honk!, Widowers' Houses (National); The Knot of the Heart, House of Games, Waste, Cloud Nine, Romance (Almeida); Serenading Louie, Be Near Me, The Chalk Garden, John Gabriel Borkman, The Cryptogram (Donmar); Love Story, Pal Joey, The Scarlet Letter, Just So (Chichester Festival Theatre); Antony and Cleopatra (Liverpool); Hello Dolly! (Regent's Park); Brian Friel's The Home Place (Gate, Dublin); Kirikou et Karaba (Casino de Paris); Apologia (Bush); The Witches of Eastwick, Donkeys' Years (UK tour), The Rivals (Bristol Old Vic), Peter Pan, The Wizard of Oz (Birmingham Rep); The Black Dahlia (Yale Repertory Company); Romeo and Juliet (Washington, DC); Me and My Girl, Fiddler on the Roof, Assassins, Ain't Misbehavin' and Guys and Dolls (Sheffield Crucible).

OPERA INCLUDES: The Handmaids' Tale (Royal Danish Opera/Canadian Opera/ENO); The Silent Twins, Love Counts (Almeida Opera).

PAUL PYANT (Lighting Designer)

RECENT THEATRE INCLUDES: Separate Tables (Chichester Festival Theatre); Another Door Closed (The Peter Hall Company at Bath Theatre Royal); The Secret Garden (West Yorkshire Playhouse); The Winter's Tale (Bridge Project at the Epidarus Festival, Greece); As You Like It, The Tempest (Bridge Project, Old Vic/New York); Waiting for Godot (West End/Australia); Enjoy (tour); Measure for Measure (RADA); True West (Sheffield Crucible); Aspects of Love (Menier Chocolate Factory). Paul has also worked extensively for Glyndebourne Opera, English National Opera, The Royal Opera House, National Theatre, English National Ballet, The Donmar Warehouse, The Almedia Theatre and Northern Ballet Theatre.

Opera work worldwide includes productions in America (Metropolitan Opera, Los Angeles, Houston, Seattle, San Francisco), Australia, New Zealand, Monte Carlo, Israel, Austria, Germany, Spain, Switzerland, Italy and Japan.

JULIET STEVENSON (Dr Diane Cassell)

FOR THE ROYAL COURT: Alice Trilogy, The Country, Death and the Maiden (& West End), Other Worlds.

OTHER THEATRE INCLUDES: Duet for One (Almeida/West End); The Seagull, Private Lives, Caucasian Chalk Circle, Hedda Gabler, Yerma (National); We Happy Few (West End); The Duchess of Malfi (Greenwich Theatre/West End); Scenes from an Execution (Mark Taper Forum, LA); Burn This (Hampstead/West End); On the Verge (Sadler's Wells); Beckett Shorts, Les Liaisons Dangereuses, As You Like It, Troilus and Cressida, Measure for Measure, A Midsummer Night's Dream, The Witch of Edmonton, Money, Henry IV Parts I and II, Once In A Lifetime, The White Guard, Hippolytus, Antony and Cleopatra, The Churchill Play, The Taming of the Shrew, The Tempest (RSC).

TELEVISION INCLUDES: Accused: Helen's Story, Dustbin Baby, Place of Execution, Ten Days to War, Hear the Silence, The Road from Coorain, The Pact, Trial By Fire, Cider with Rosie, Stone Scissors Paper, The Politician's Wife, Out of Love, Stanley, The March, A Doll's House, Life Story, Antigone, Oedipus at Colonus, Freud, Bazaar and Rummage, The Mallens, Maybury.

FILM INCLUDES: Desert Flower, The Secret Of Moonacre, And When Did You Last See Your Father?, Breaking and Entering, Pierrepoint, The Snow Queen, A Previous Engagement, Infamous, Being Julia, Mona Lisa Smile, Nicholas Nickleby, Food for Love, Bend It Like Beckham, Emma, A Secret Rapture, Who Dealt, The Trial, Truly Madly Deeply, Ladder Of Swords, Drowning By Numbers.

AWARDS INCLUDE: 2009 Golden Dagger Best Actress Award and LA Drama Critics' Circle Best Actress Award for Place of Execution, 2002 AFI Best Actress in a Television Drama for The Road from Coorain, 2002 National Board of Review Best Acting by an Ensemble for Nicholas Nickleby, 1996 BAFTA Best Actress Award for The Politician's Wife, 1992 Time Out Best Actress Award and Laurence Olivier Best Actress Award for Death and the Maiden, 1990 Evening Standard Best Actress Award for Truly, Madly, Deeply, ACE Cable TV Network Best Supporting Actress Award for Life Story, Laurence Olivier Best Actress Award for Yerma.

LEAH WHITAKER (Catherine Tickell)

THEATRE INCLUDES: Counted (UK tour); Pride and Prejudice (Bath Theatre Royal/tour); Found in the Ground (Wrestling School); Harvest (Oxford Playhouse/tour).

TELEVISION: Midsomer Murders.

LYDIA WILSON (Phoebe)

THEATRE INCLUDES: Blasted (Lyric Hammersmith); Pains of Youth (National); The House of Special Purpose (Chichester Festival Theatre).

TELEVISION INCLUDES: South Riding, Crimson Petal and the White, Any Human Heart, Pete Versus Life, Midsomer Murders.

FILM: Never Let Me Go.

THE ENGLISH STAGE COMPANY
AT THE ROYAL COURT THEATRE

'For me the theatre is really a religion or way of life. You must decide what you feel the world is about and what you want to say about it, so that everything in the theatre you work in is saying the same thing ... A theatre must have a recognisable attitude. It will have one, whether you like it or not.'

George Devine, first artistic director of the English Stage Company: notes for an unwritten book.

photo: Stephen Cummiskey

As Britain's leading national company dedicated to new work, the Royal Court Theatre produces new plays of the highest quality, working with writers from all backgrounds, and asking questions about who we are and the world in which we live.

"The Royal Court has been at the centre of British cultural life for the past 50 years, an engine room for new writing and constantly transforming the theatrical culture." Stephen Daldry

Since its foundation in 1956, the Royal Court has presented premieres by almost every leading contemporary British playwright, from John Osborne's Look Back in Anger to Caryl Churchill's A Number and Tom Stoppard's Rock 'n' Roll. Just some of the other writers to have chosen the Royal Court to premiere their work include Edward Albee, John Arden, Richard Bean, Samuel Beckett, Edward Bond, Leo Butler, Jez Butterworth, Martin Crimp, Ariel Dorfman, Stella Feehily, Christopher Hampton, David Hare, Eugène Ionesco, Ann Jellicoe, Terry Johnson, Sarah Kane, David Mamet, Martin McDonagh, Conor McPherson, Joe Penhall, Lucy Prebble, Mark Ravenhill, Simon Stephens, Wole Soyinka, Polly Stenham, David Storey, Debbie Tucker Green, Arnold Wesker and Roy Williams.

"It is risky to miss a production there." Financial Times

In addition to its full-scale productions, the Royal Court also facilitates international work at a grass roots level, developing exchanges which bring young writers to Britain and sending British writers, actors and directors to work with artists around the world. The research and play development arm of the Royal Court Theatre, The Studio, finds the most exciting and diverse range of new voices in the UK. The Studio runs playwriting groups including the Young Writers Programme, Critical Mass for black, Asian and minority ethnic writers and the biennial Young Writers Festival. For further information, go to www.royalcourttheatre.com/ywp.

"Yes, the Royal Court is on a roll. Yes, Dominic Cooke has just the genius and kick that this venue needs... It's fist-bitingly exciting." Independent

MAKING IT HAPPEN

The Royal Court develops and produces more new plays than any other national theatre in the UK. To produce such a broad and eclectic programme and all of our play development activities costs over £5 million every year. Just under half of this is met by principal funding from Arts Council England. The rest must be found from box office income, trading and financial support from private individuals, companies and charitable foundations. The Royal Court is a registered charity (231242) and grateful for every donation it receives towards its work.

You can support the theatre by joining one of its membership schemes or by making a donation towards the Writers Development Fund. The Fund underpins all of the work that the Royal Court undertakes with new and emerging playwrights across the globe, giving them the tools and opportunities to flourish.

To find out how to become involved with the Royal Court and the difference that your support could make visit www.royalcourttheatre.com/support-us or call the Development Office on 020 7565 5049.

MAJOR PARTNERSHIPS

The Royal Court is able to offer its unique playwriting and audience development programmes because of significant and longstanding partnerships with the organisations that support it.

Principal funding is received from Arts Council England. The Genesis Foundation supports the Royal Court's work with International Playwrights. Theatre Local is sponsored by Bloomberg. The Jerwood Charitable Foundation supports new plays by playwrights through the Jerwood New Playwrights series. The Artistic Director's Chair is supported by a lead grant from The Peter Jay Sharp Foundation, contributing to the activities of the Artistic Director's office. Over the past ten years the BBC has supported the Gerald Chapman Fund for directors.

DEVELOPMENT ADVOCATES

John Ayton
Elizabeth Bandeen
Tim Blythe
Anthony Burton
Sindy Caplan
Cas Donald (Vice Chair)
Allie Esiri
Celeste Fenichel
Anoushka Healy
Emma Marsh (Chair)
Mark Robinson
William Russell
Deborah Shaw Marquardt (Vice Chair)
Nick Wheeler
Daniel Winterfeldt

Supported by
ARTS COUNCIL ENGLAND

PROGRAMME SUPPORTERS

PUBLIC FUNDING
Arts Council England, London
British Council
European Commission
Representation in the UK
New Deal of the Mind

CHARITABLE DONATIONS
American Friends of the
Royal Court Theatre
The Brim Foundation*
Gerald Chapman Fund
City Bridge Trust
Columbia Foundation
Cowley Charitable Trust
The Dorset Foundation
Do Well Foundation Ltd*
The Edmond de Rothschild
Foundation*
The John Ellerman Foundation
The Epstein Parton
Foundation*
The Eranda Foundation
Frederick Loewe Foundation*
Genesis Foundation
The Golden Bottle Trust
The Goldsmiths' Company
The H & G de Freitas
Charitable Trust
Haberdashers' Company
Jerwood Charitable
Foundation
John Thaw Foundation
John Lyon's Charity
J Paul Getty Jnr Charitable
Trust
The Laura Pels Foundation*
Leathersellers' Company
Marina Kleinwort Charitable
Trust
The Martin Bowley
Charitable Trust
The Andrew W. Mellon
Foundation
Paul Hamlyn Foundation
Jerome Robbins Foundation*
Rose Foundation
Rosenkranz Foundation
Royal Victoria Hall Foundation
The Peter Jay Sharp
Foundation*
The Steel Charitable Trust

CORPORATE SUPPORTERS & SPONSORS
BBC
Bloomberg
Coutts & Co
Ecosse Films
French Wines
Grey London
Gymbox
Kudos Film & Television
MAC
Moët & Chandon
Smythson of Bond Street

BUSINESS ASSOCIATES, MEMBERS & BENEFACTORS
Auerbach & Steele Opticians
Bank of America Merrill Lynch
Hugo Boss
Lazard
Oberon Books
Vanity Fair

INDIVIDUAL MEMBERS
ICE-BREAKERS
Anonymous
Rosemary Alexander
Lisa & Andrew Barnett
Mrs Renate Blackwood
Ossi & Paul Burger
Mrs Helena Butler
Lindsey Carlon
Mr Claes Hesselgren & Mrs
Jane Collins
Mark & Tobey Dichter
Ms P Dolphin
Elizabeth & James Downing
Virginia Finegold
Charlotte & Nick Fraser
Mark & Rebecca Goldbart
Alastair & Lynwen Gibbons
Mr & Mrs Green
Sebastian & Rachel Grigg
Mrs Hattrell
Stephen & Candice Hurwitz
Mrs R Jay
David Lanch
Yasmine Lever
Colette & Peter Levy
Watcyn Lewis
Mr & Mrs Peter Lord
David Marks QC
Nicola McFarland
Jonathan & Edward Mills
Ann Norman-Butler
Emma O'Donoghue
Mrs Georgia Oetker
Janet & Michael Orr
Pauline Pinder
Mr & Mrs William Poeton
The Really Useful Group
Mr & Mrs Tim Reid
Lois Sieff OBE
Nick & Louise Steidl
Torsten Thiele
Laura & Stephen Zimmerman

GROUND-BREAKERS
Anonymous
Moira Andreae
Nick Archdale
Charlotte Asprey
Jane Attias*
Caroline Baker
Brian Balfour-Oatts
Elizabeth & Adam Bandeen
Ray Barrell
Dr Kate Best
Philip Blackwell
Stan & Val Bond
Neil & Sarah Brener

Miss Deborah Brett
Sindy & Jonathan Caplan
Gavin & Lesley Casey
Sarah & Philippe Chappatte
Tim & Caroline Clark
Carole & Neville Conrad
Kay Ellen Consolver
Clyde Cooper
Ian & Caroline Cormack
Mr & Mrs Cross
Andrew & Amanda Cryer
Alison Davies
Noel De Keyzer
Rob & Cherry Dickins
Denise & Randolph Dumas
Robyn Durie
Glenn & Phyllida Earle
Margaret Exley CBE
Allie Esiri
Celeste & Peter Fenichel
Margy Fenwick
Tim Fosberry
The Edwin Fox Foundation
John Garfield
Beverley Gee
Mr & Mrs Georgiades
Nick & Julie Gould
Lord & Lady Grabiner
Richard & Marcia Grand*
Nick Gray
Reade & Elizabeth Griffith
Don & Sue Guiney
Jill Hackel & Andrzej Zarzycki
Douglas & Mary Hampson
Sally Hampton
Sam & Caroline Haubold
Anoushka Healy
Mr & Mrs J Hewett
Gordon Holmes
The David Hyman Charitable
Trust
Mrs Madeleine Inkin
Nicholas Jones
Nicholas Josefowitz
Dr Evi Kaplanis
David P Kaskel & Christopher
A Teano
Vincent & Amanda Keaveny
Peter & Maria Kellner*
Steve Kingshott
Mrs Joan Kingsley &
Mr Philip Kingsley
Mr & Mrs Pawel Kisielewski
Maria Lam
Larry & Peggy Levy
Daisy & Richard Littler
Kathryn Ludlow
David & Elizabeth Miles
Barbara Minto
Ann & Gavin Neath CBE
The North Street Trust
Murray North
Clive & Annie Norton
William Plapinger & Cassie
Murray*
Andrea & Hilary Ponti
Wendy & Philip Press

Serena Prest
Julie Ritter
Paul & Gill Robinson
Mark & Tricia Robinson
Paul & Jill Ruddock
William & Hilary Russell
Julie & Bill Ryan
Sally & Anthony Salz
Bhags Sharma
Mrs Doris Sherwood
The Michael & Melanie
Sherwood Foundation
Tom Siebens & Mimi Parsons
Anthony Simpson & Susan
Boster
Richard Simpson
Brian D Smith
Samantha & Darren Smith
The Ulrich Family
The Ury Trust
Mr & Mrs Nick Wheeler
Sian & Matthew Westerman
Carol Woolton
Katherine & Michael Yates*

BOUNDARY-BREAKERS
Katie Bradford
Lydia & Manfred Gorvy
Ms Alex Joffe
Emma Marsh

MOVER-SHAKERS
Anonymous
John and Annoushka Ayton
Cas & Philip Donald
Lloyd & Sarah Dorfman
Duncan Matthews QC
The David & Elaine Potter
Foundation
Ian & Carol Sellars
Edgar & Judith Wallner

HISTORY-MAKERS
Eric Abraham & Sigrid Rausing
Miles Morland

MAJOR DONORS
Rob & Siri Cope
Daniel & Joanna Friel
Jack & Linda Keenan*
Deborah & Stephen
Marquardt
Lady Sainsbury of Turville
NoraLee & Jon Sedmak*
Jan & Michael Topham
The Williams Charitable Trust

*Supporters of the American
Friends of the Royal Court
(AFRCT)

FOR THE ROYAL COURT

Royal Court Theatre, Sloane Square, London SW1W 8AS
Tel: 020 7565 5050 Fax: 020 7565 5001
info@royalcourttheatre.com, www.royalcourttheatre.com

THE HERETIC

Richard Bean

THE HERETIC

OBERON BOOKS
LONDON

First published in 2011 by Oberon Books Ltd
521 Caledonian Road, London N7 9RH
Tel: 020 7607 3637 / Fax: 020 7607 3629
e-mail: info@oberonbooks.com
www.oberonbooks.com

A catalogue record for this book is available from the British
Library.

ISBN: 978-1-84943-120-0

Cover image by feastcreative.com

Printed in Great Britain by CPI Antony Rowe, Chippenham.

I'd like to thank the following for their help and support in developing the script. Chris Campbell, Erica Whyman, Sonia Friedman, Jack Bradley, Dominic Cooke, James Fleet, Clive Coleman, Martin Wright, Jeremy Herrin, Lisa Makin, Dr Stewart Bean, Adrian Hood and Jemma Kennedy. And all the cast who have made contributions along the way. Thank you.

Richard Bean

"We are dealing with a coupled non-linear chaotic system, and therefore the long-term prediction of future climate states is not possible."

Intergovernmental Panel on Climate Change
(Third Assessment Report)

"The science is settled."
Al Gore

Characters

DR. DIANE CASSELL 40s
(Palaeogeophysics and Geodynamics lecturer)

BEN SHOTTER 19
(an Earth Sciences undergraduate)

PHOEBE 21
(Dr. Cassell's daughter)

GEOFF TORDOFF 40s
(Site Services for the University Campus, with a
brief for Security)

PROFESSOR KEVIN MALONEY 50s
(Head of Faculty Earth Sciences)

CATHERINE TICKELL 20s
(Human Resources Officer)

SET

A modern university head of department office. Desk, chair, computer, book shelves, cabinets. A circle of six comfy chairs (dull functional designs, this is not Oxbridge) are set around a coffee table for tutorials. A whiteboard with some climate change algorithms of a difficult, and mathematical nature. The words "infrared", "radiation", "forcing" and "feedback" feature.

On the wall a series of photos. The first is of a six-year-old girl (Phoebe) standing next to a sapling Betel Nut tree. The second when she is about fourteen and the tree bigger. The photos are taken in the Maldives on the wash limit of the sea.

For Acts 4 and 5 the set is Diane's kitchen in the country.

Act One

SCENE ONE

(A September morning. DIANE is mounting a photograph of a Betel Nut tree taken on the wash limit on a Maldives beach. She hangs it next to seven other photos of the same tree making a series. PHOEBE stands in front of the first in the series.)

PHOEBE: This has just godda be illegal.

DIANE: What?

PHOEBE: Having a photograph of this four-year-old girl on your wall, in a bikini.

DIANE: *(A loud sigh.)*

PHOEBE: Stop sighing mum. You sound like you're in The Archers. Making jam. Or getting raped. From behind. By Jack Woolley.

DIANE: Don't make jokes about Jack Woolley. He's got Alzheimer's.

PHOEBE: Exactly, he thinks you're Peggy.

DIANE: The subject of the photograph is the tree.

PHOEBE: A paedophile would not even notice the tree. *And* I look fat.

DIANE: I know, but you've lost weight since then.

PHOEBE: Bitch. Give me a pen.

DIANE: Get your own pen. There's some about two yards over there.

PHOEBE: Fascist. You're wasted in this job, you could be running Burma.

(PHOEBE gets the pen. There is a knock at the door.)

DIANE: Come in!

(Enter BEN. His T-shirt bears the slogan FUCK. He carries a cycle seat.)

Hello.

BEN: Yeah.

DIANE: I'm Doctor Cassell. There are no tutorials in Freshers' week. Are you one of mine? PaleoGeophysics?

BEN: Yeah.

DIANE: What's your name?

BEN: Ben Shotter.

DIANE: Can I help?

BEN: Next Tuesday, yeah, we got the trip to the weather station by mini-bus, yeah, on the Tuesday, yeah, but the modular lecture's in the morning.

DIANE: At eleven o'clock. Yes.

BEN: Which is like course assessed yeah?

PHOEBE: Uurgh. How long's this gonna take?!

BEN: I can't, like, do them both on the same day.

PHOEBE: You haven't got the energy?

DIANE: Phoebe! Please!

BEN: I can't travel by mini-bus.

DIANE: What have you got against mini-buses?

BEN: It depends what kind of mini-bus it is?

DIANE: I think it's a Toyota.

PHOEBE: Ugh. Is it petrol or diesel?

DIANE: It's going to be one or the other isn't it.

PHOEBE: Muslims and Jews can't eat pork. He can't get on a fossil fuels mini-bus.

BEN: Yeah.

DIANE: So how are you going to get to the weather station?

BEN: I'm gonna have to like cycle.

DIANE: It's forty miles. There. And forty miles back.

BEN: Yeah, I'll set off like really early.

PHOEBE: He's trying to tell you that he'll miss the modular lecture.

DIANE: Attendance at the modular lecture is part of the first year continuous assessment. It's worth two credits.

BEN: That's my point.

DIANE: You're going to miss out on two course work credits then, aren't you.

BEN: Harsh man.

PHOEBE: *(To DIANE.)* That's religious discrimination.

(To BEN.) Do you believe in God?

BEN: No.

PHOEBE: I do. Rather controversially I believe that God is an old man with a white beard sitting on a cloud.

BEN: *(To PHOEBE.)* Are you a Fresher?

PHOEBE: Do I look like a Fresher?

BEN: You're not a student?

PHOEBE: No. I'm a farm worker. I drive a tractor.

DIANE: One day a week. In order to consolidate our travel, every Tuesday, I give my daughter a lift into York, in a petrol driven car.

BEN: Why do you have to be in York at all?

DIANE: There's an essential thing we do together on a Tuesday lunchtime.

PHOEBE: Mad club.

DIANE: Family therapy. And we don't mind anybody knowing about it.

PHOEBE: That's how mad we are.

BEN: I've had aversion therapy.

PHOEBE: Did it work?

BEN: No.

PHOEBE: How old are you?

DIANE: Phoebe?!

BEN: Nineteen. I took a year off.

DIANE: What did you do?

BEN: Nothing, like I said, I took a year off.

DIANE: In your green future how would we get fourteen students fifty miles to the North Yorkshire Moors' weather station?

BEN: There should be like an electric car / mini-bus.

DIANE: OK. This is your first assignment. For next week compare the energy efficiency and emissions of an electric car and a diesel car.

BEN: Electric cars don't have any emissions.

DIANE: Electric cars should be called coal cars. 30% of our energy comes from coal. Electricity is not naturally occurring in nature.

BEN: There's eels.

DIANE: Eels?

BEN: Electric eels.

PHOEBE: Yeah, good point.

DIANE: If you want to pursue this argument you'll need to write a letter to Professor Kevin Maloney, Faculty of Earth Sciences.

BEN: Cool. Ta.

DIANE: See you next week.

(He studies the photo of PHOEBE as a four-year-old in a bikini. Then he looks at PHOEBE.)

PHOEBE: What?

BEN: Nothing. Laters.

(He turns to go. The back of his T-shirt bears the slogan OFF. DIANE closes the door.)

PHOEBE: He's really cute.

DIANE: Why is it young women can't resist hopeless romantic visionaries?

PHOEBE: I can and I do. Regularly.

DIANE: That Buddhist monk in the Maldives. He changed your life.

PHOEBE: No he didn't.

DIANE: You'd never had a yeast infection before.

PHOEBE: One area which is not legitimate source material for your pathetic comedy quipping is the medical history of my vagina.

DIANE: Have you joined up then? Are you going to *get active*?

PHOEBE: Yeah. I have. They have a branch in Scarborough.

DIANE: How are you going to get to Scarborough?

PHOEBE: I don't know. Yet. Why do you hate them so much?

DIANE: Because they're bad people.

PHOEBE: They don't sound like bad people. Greeeeenpeeeeeace.

DIANE: Are you joining Greenpeace to save the world or as part of your ongoing project to destroy your mother?

PHOEBE: Can I let you know tomorrow?

DIANE: Come on! I need to eat and you need to eat and throw up, which takes longer.

PHOEBE: I've eaten.

DIANE: Nothing tastes as good as skinny feels.

(They exit, the door is closed.)

End of Scene.

SCENE TWO

(The next day. GEOFF and DIANE. GEOFF is wearing a cheapish suit with a high vis waistcoat over. He has the trappings of a security guard – boots, name badge, keys, two way radio etc. He has an envelope, and its contents in his hand. DIANE is seated on the edge of her desk.)

GEOFF: I can't see that there's owt worth worrying about here.

DIANE: It's a death threat.

GEOFF: Yeah, but –

DIANE: – yeah but?

GEOFF: It's Freshers' week.

(Beat.) Last night one of the rugby lads got pissed and bit the head off a grey squirrel. Knowhatimean?

DIANE: I do know what you mean. Half a bottle of Pinot Grigio, and I'm out there myself, on my hands and knees, chewing the heads off rodents.

GEOFF: I coulda called the police, but it woulda ruined the lad's career.

DIANE: What's he want to be?

GEOFF: A vet. I'll have a dig around. After I got mesen decommissioned I did a bit of freelance private eyeing.

DIANE: You were in the army were you Geoff?

GEOFF: Marines. Oh aye, I can kill a man with my bare hands.

DIANE: You must give me your card.

(GEOFF gives her a card.)

First aider too. So you can kill and heal. That's quite a broad vocation.

GEOFF: Have you gone and got yersen you know, whatsaname… with a student?

DIANE: I've never had sex with any of my students.

GEOFF: Can you think of any reason why these radical greens, The Sacred Earth Militia, would want to put a death threat on the windscreen of your four litre, eight cylinder Jaguar XK8?

DIANE: No idea.

GEOFF: You could have that car converted to liquid petroleum gas.

(GEOFF gives her a brochure for a garage.)

This is an accredited conversion centre. They did all my site services vehicles. Ask for Karl. Opposite The Waggoners Rest in Pocklington. That's your side o' town int'it?

DIANE: Yes.

(Enter PROFESSOR KEVIN MALONEY.)

KEVIN: Sorry I'm late. Ran over a cat. Are you alright Geoff?

GEOFF: Dunno. I never think about it. What about you Professor?

KEVIN: Upset, obviously, about the cat. It's Mrs Nextdoor's.

DIANE: I've had a death threat from "The Sacred Earth Militia".

KEVIN: Oh dear. Hell's bells.

(GEOFF hands over the envelope.)

"All heretic's must die". Ah! Elementary, my dear Watson! Misuse of the possessive apostrophe, incorrectly placed after the C of heretic and before the S.

GEOFF: So what does that tell us?

DIANE: Our suspect is a greengrocer.

GEOFF: It's godda be someone on campus. Staff or student.

DIANE: Geoff has established that I've not had sex with any of my students.

KEVIN: I don't blame you. *(To GEOFF.)* Have you seen them? Kaw!

DIANE: Intimate relations with colleagues is next.

KEVIN: That was twenty years ago. *(To GEOFF.)* Isafjord, Iceland.

DIANE: He put his hands up my jumper.

KEVIN: *(To GEOFF.)* I can explain.

GEOFF: Go on then.

KEVIN: My hands were cold.

GEOFF: I haven't told the Old Bill about the death threat. I like to keep –

DIANE: – I'm sorry Geoff! But I insist that we go to the police.

GEOFF: I'll talk to my mate Dave in Special Branch.

DIANE: You've got direct access to Special Branch?

GEOFF: Yeah. When we had them Muslim nutters on campus Al whatsaname –

KEVIN: – Al-Muhajiroun. Arabic Studies' Doctor Mukarjee had three death threats. He'd said there were some grammatical errors in the Koran.

DIANE: Maybe Arabic is Allah's second language.

GEOFF: *(Knowing.)* So what's his first?

DIANE: – Hebrew. I see the problem.

GEOFF: Professor Maloney's parking place is scanned by cctv. Swap with the Professor we can candid camera the little bugger.

KEVIN: Brilliant! I'll move my car. Where do you want me to park?

DIANE: Between the kitchen bins and the builders' skips.

KEVIN: Excellent.

GEOFF: Give me your keys, I'll move the cars for you now.

DIANE: No, that's alright Geoff, I'll − (pop out)

GEOFF: − Site Services mission statement is to "facilitate excellence". Apparently that's your excellence not mine. I'll get your keys back to you by dinner time, don't panic, dinner time is Yorkshire for lunchtime.

(DIANE and GEOFF hand over their keys.)

KEVIN: Geoff, I got a letter from one of Diane's first year PaleoGs, said he couldn't get on the bus to the weather station, it's against his principles.

GEOFF: What's his name?

DIANE: Ben Shotter.

GEOFF: I'll get Special Branch Dave to check him out.

KEVIN: Can your brother-in-law do an LPG conversion on a Jag?

DIANE: Oh it's your brother-in-law!

KEVIN: Half the price of petrol, and no pollution. They did mine.

DIANE: Kevin, your car is a Toyota Prius.

KEVIN: First one they've ever done. If you got the Jag converted, you get a little LPG sticker. That might put an end to all this.

DIANE: Has Doctor Mukarjee started to wear a burka?

GEOFF: It's worth considering, love. We all have to try and reduce our carbon footprints. You've got children. This is your daughter innit?

DIANE: Yes.

GEOFF: Aye, well then. The future in't ours is it, it's theirs.

(GEOFF is heading for the door when he spots a desk lamp that has been left on.)

Do you want this on?

(No one answers, he turns it off and leaves closing the door behind him. KEVIN tries to give DIANE the bound document. She's not interested.)

KEVIN: My draft IPCC chapter.

DIANE: You want me to read it, make some intelligent comments which you can pass off as your own, in order to enhance your international reputation.

KEVIN: Yeah.

DIANE: Kevin, I've had a death threat.

KEVIN: Sorry. Yes, mmm, terrible.

(He puts the document down and tries to care.)

DIANE: I don't know whether I should tell Phoebe about the death threat. Any stress, like this and –

KEVIN: – I've never properly understood anorexia, is it real, or –

DIANE: – it's the physical expression of self obsession, that's what it is.

KEVIN: Psychosomatic?

DIANE: Laboratory experiments on mice suggest a genetic root, which suits Phoebe because that means it's my fault. I have an alternative theory – they bought a batch of really fucking selfish mice.

KEVIN: Has she got a boyfriend?

DIANE: Sex does not cure anorexia.

KEVIN: You say that, but in "Cuckoo's Nest" Jack Nicholson fixes up B b b b b billy with a girl, and he is cured of his stammer. How ill can anyone be if they're getting a regular sorting out?

DIANE: Kevin! You're talking about my daughter.

KEVIN: Sorry.

DIANE: Have you ever had a death threat?

KEVIN: Yes. Last year.

DIANE: From whom?

KEVIN: Gordon Brown. "Kevin" he said, "you promised me my children would never see a white Christmas. So how come Scotland's cut off and I'm digging them out of a twenty foot snow drift." I said "Ah! Not my fault, Prime Minister, I'm your *climate* expert, that snow is *weather*."

DIANE: Ha! Brilliant!

KEVIN: He called me a wanker.

(Beat. KEVIN sighs, looks needy.)

DIANE: Are you alright Kevin?

KEVIN: Sabina. Big row, in the car, coming back from Caroline Spelman's fish pie dinner. First she accused me of flirting with Theresa May.

DIANE: Were you?

KEVIN: Obviously. But… Sabina said I was "tedious". That's not a good word to use in a marriage about the person you're married to is it – tedious. I stopped the car and said "only boring people get bored".

DIANE: Ah, that was the right thing to say.

(KEVIN sighs, stands and closely inspects the new photo of the Betel Nut tree.)

KEVIN: Don't you get bored measuring sea level?

RICHARD BEAN

DIANE: In the Maldives?

KEVIN: This tree you planted is still doing well then?

DIANE: Yes.

KEVIN: What –

DIANE: – it's a Betel Nut tree. No saline tolerance. I planted it – you know all this – on the wash limit sixteen years ago, and it's thriving.

KEVIN: So is sea level rising in the Maldives?

DIANE: Technically, no.

KEVIN: No rise and no rising trend?

DIANE: No rising trend.

KEVIN: Mm. Have you written your paper?

DIANE: Yes.

KEVIN: Have you submitted? Which journal? Nature?

DIANE: Yes Nature, no, not yet. What is this?

KEVIN: So Toby's not read it yet?

DIANE: No.

(KEVIN sits.)

You've sat down. You only sit down when you're angry.

KEVIN: We need a new "business model" for this department.

DIANE: I thought I worked at a university.

KEVIN: After Christmas we're getting a visit from Catalan International Securities. Have you heard of them?

DIANE: Are they Quakers?

KEVIN: One of the biggest insurance and underwriting firms in Europe.

DIANE: Oh yes. They sponsored that mad person who tried to pedalo across the Arctic to show how radical the melt was.

He got stuck in pack ice and the dogs had to shoot him and eat him.

KEVIN: Yes that's them. For Catalan, that was a PR disaster. For us, good news. Now they're prepared to pay a very high price to be advised by the best.

DIANE: You and me.

KEVIN: The "Climate Change Research Unit" would service clients by –

DIANE: – I'm not a sex worker.

KEVIN: Listen! We are the Earth Sciences Faculty of YUIST for teaching, but *virtually* we are a separate budget centre, providing tools to the market.

DIANE: What tools would I be selling?

KEVIN: A computer model of sea level rise.

DIANE: I'd rather sell the fluff from my naval. It'd be more use. After a couple of years they could knit a jumper.

KEVIN: Catalan... how can I explain... there's a Chinese proverb. "Man must stand for long time, with mouth open, before roast duck fly in".

DIANE: If I were Catalan I'd go to Hampshire University.

KEVIN: Hampshire is the competition, but they've got all their eggs in one basket, tree ring research. We have me, ice cores, glaciers; you, sea level; Doctor Popodopolos – what does he do?

DIANE: I don't know.

KEVIN: We have intellectual diversity.

DIANE: It would help if Catalan were not aware of the sceptical nature of the sea level expert's views.

KEVIN: And that sea level expert will agree to delay the publication of her latest paper until after the Catalan decision.

DIANE: You're telling me not to publish my research?

KEVIN: I'm telling you to delay the publication of your research.

DIANE: I don't understand. Last year, when we were a designated "Centre of Excellence" you told me that I needed to publish more.

(Standing excitedly.)

KEVIN: I didn't want to be a "centre of fucking excellence" I was happy being a "centre of ducking and diving and falling asleep in the afternoons". But the good old days of being funded from Central Government are dead and fucking buried. And, I now understand that, like everyone, I am only two bad mistakes away from driving a mini-cab for a living.

DIANE: OK. I will not submit my paper to Nature until after the Catalan decision.

KEVIN: End of Jan. Goodo.

(He stands.)

I'll go and see Miss Tickle in Human Resources, see what we need to do about this death threat.

DIANE: Miss Tickle? Is she new?

KEVIN: Yes. She ran this "line manager's course" during the summer. She introduced herself as having worked for Mars for six years. I said "don't expect us to be impressed because you've worked for a local authority". Tumbleweed. Disciplinarian, wears a lot of leather. Looks like the kind of woman who might collect Nazi memorabilia.

(KEVIN stands and heads for the door.)

Got the Vice Chancellor at eleven, something about women. Exciting though isn't it. I love September. And Earth Sciences has been ignored for so long, but now, suddenly, the kids think we're cool.

DIANE: Get out Kevin, I might hurl.

KEVIN: It was the Arts forever, wasn't it, until in the sixties Sociology floated to the top like an aerated turd, hung around for a few years, before finally getting sucked down the tube of its own gaping fatuousness. Then in the seventies, the Psychologists took over the asylum. Boy did those tossers fancy themselves. But they could never nail anything properly down. One minute being mentally ill is a crushing personal tragedy, next minute it's a bit of a laugh and you should try to enjoy it. All that Psychology ever achieved was making bullshit respectable, which of course, paved the way for Media Studies and ten years' of mind-numbing bollocks! So that day, last year, when Media Studies' top witch knocked on my door and begged me to let her first years on to your introductory Earth Sciences modular lecture, that was the moment I knew we'd finally arrived. It's official – we are the kings of the castle. Let's not fuck it up eh!

(He closes the door.)

End of Scene.

SCENE THREE

(Second week of term. DIANE's office on campus. BEN sits diagonally across from DIANE in an easy chair. Next to him is a bass guitar case with THE FOUR HORSEMEN stencilled on it.)

DIANE: I can smell garlic.

BEN: That'll be me. I eat a lot of garlic.

DIANE: Is eating garlic a Death Metal ordinance?

BEN: *(Sighing.)* Tut.

DIANE: Your band, The Four Horsemen, they're not a Death Metal band?

BEN: *(Sighing.)* Tut.

DIANE: What other music genres do I know? Grime?

BEN: *(Exasperated.)* Tut. Man, who likes Grime?

DIANE: I don't like grime. I pay a cleaner. Ben, if you want to be a rock star you should be at art college.

BEN: So you're gonna lay on the stress now, yeah?

DIANE: Stress? In Pol Pot's Cambodia, students like you were executed. Why do you think there has never been a single decent Cambodian rock band?

BEN: You're a denier. Right?

DIANE: Holocaust or –

BEN: *(Sighing.)* – Tut. *Anthropogenic global warming.*

DIANE: I'm agnostic on *AGW*, but if you can prove to me there's a God I'll become a nun quicker than you can say "lesbian convent orgy".

BEN: That's sexist.

DIANE: No.

BEN: Homophobic.

DIANE: Yes. Semantic specificity is the E chord of science.

BEN: Are you allowed to be homophobic in a government funded educational establishment, in the, like, you know, public sector?

DIANE: I doubt it. Why did you choose Earth Sciences?

BEN: *(Knowing.)* I wanna save the planet innit.

DIANE: The planet doesn't need saving. The planet will be fine. You mean you'd like to save the human race.

BEN: Whatever.

DIANE: I'm a scientist. I'm not a politician.

BEN: You're saying that, like, I can't be a scientist, and an activist?

DIANE: Activism and Empiricism are opposites.

BEN: Do you know a good art college?

DIANE: My job is to make you think like a scientist. You need to be aware of your agenda or leave it at home.

BEN: I don't understand.

DIANE: OK. I would say that the repressed homosexual Baden Powell started the Boy Scout movement on the energy of an unacknowledged agenda.

BEN: If he'd been aware of what he was really after, he'd have set up Gaydar.

DIANE: Yup.

BEN: Or Grindr.

DIANE: What's Grindr?

BEN: It's a gay app utilising like GPS satellite technology that tells you if there's another gay guy within twenty yards of you who's up for sex.

DIANE: You're gay?

BEN: No, but I am passionate about developments in mobile computing.

DIANE: Let's do some politics disguised as climate science.

(DIANE gives him a whiteboard pen.)

You work for Greenpeace. Illustrate the rise in CO_2 since 1800 on the whiteboard.

BEN: My agenda would be to try and make it look scary.

DIANE: Scare me.

(BEN stands at the whiteboard and draws in the x axis writing in the dates.)

BEN: So x axis is 1800 to 2000. y axis is 280 parts per million to 380 parts per million. So the rise in CO_2 since industrialisation is – scary.

(BEN draws in a line basically joining the bottom left to the top right in a 45° angle.)

DIANE: Excellent. Now you work for Exxon Mobil. Reassure me that driving my car is not a problem.

BEN: I'd want to show a flat line, right along the bottom. Er… I'd change the y axis, make the y axis percentages, so 0% to 5%, then CO_2 in 1800 is 0.028 percent rising to 0.038.

(He draws a flat line across the bottom of the whiteboard.)

– a flat line, across the bottom. Nothing to worry about.

DIANE: And which one is correct?

BEN: They're both correct. That's your point lady.

DIANE: You know for most students I have to draw those graphs.

BEN: Yeah? Why?

DIANE: I admire your passion, your idealism, your cycling. My only fear is that your faith will corrupt your science. So, do you want to go to art college?

BEN: No. I never did. That was your idea.

DIANE: Good. Do you cycle from York to your parents? Brighton isn't it?

BEN: My mother's dead.

DIANE: I'm sorry.

BEN: I killed her.

DIANE: She died in child birth?

BEN: You get one point lady.

DIANE: But your father's alive?

BEN: I hate him.

DIANE: Why?

BEN: He drives a Volvo.

DIANE: What have you got against CO_2?

BEN: It's the major greenhouse gas –

DIANE: – the major greenhouse gas is water vapour.

BEN: CO_2 destroyed Venus.

DIANE: Venus has two hundred and thirty thousand times as much CO_2.

BEN: Look, if we double CO_2, we double temperatures, that's bare bait man, and that is the end of the world. Common sense innit.

DIANE: If common sense trumped science my mother would be running a nuclear power station. The relationship between CO_2 and temperature is not linear, it's logarithmic. Think of an example, from your own life perhaps, where doubling a variable does not double the effect.

BEN: Now?

DIANE: Yes now, time's running out, apparently.

(Silence. He thinks hard.)

BEN: If you're depressed, yeah, and you buy a dog, that might make you + 3 happier. If you *double* the number of dogs, that wouldn't *double* your happiness, 'cause the second dog, because it knows it is *"the second dog"* would develop psychological problems and start pooing on your head, and that, and you would consider having it put down, which makes you feel guilty, so you start self harming, and drinking, secretly, which means you neglect the dogs, and in the end the RSPCA break the door down, take both dogs off you, and you're back to where you started. Depressed, on your own, only it's worse this time 'cause you got no front door.

DIANE: For next time, you are Archimedes, observe the world, find an example, not dogs, of a variable which when doubled doesn't have a doubling effect.

BEN: *Homework?*

DIANE: Yup.

(BEN stands. Makes to leave.)

BEN: Is Phoebe in today?

DIANE: She only comes into York on a Tuesday.

BEN: I couldn't find any Phoebe Cassell on Facebook.

DIANE: She uses her father's surname.

BEN: What's her father's name?

(Silence.)

DIANE: Gallagher.

BEN: Safe. Cool. I like you.

(He leaves. She shuts the door behind him.)

End of Scene.

Act Two

SCENE ONE

(Mid term. KEVIN, GEOFF and DIANE. It's colder now, and GEOFF is wearing a high vis coat. KEVIN is also wearing a winter coat. KEVIN is reading a second death threat.)

KEVIN: *(Reading.)* "The earth's future is more important than one human life".

Ah! This time, correct use of the apostrophe!

GEOFF: So what – probably a different perpetrator?

DIANE: Or it could be the same person who's been on a course.

KEVIN: Was it on the windscreen again?

DIANE: It was in the car.

KEVIN: They broke into the car?

GEOFF: They smashed the windscreen.

KEVIN: Hell's bells.

GEOFF: Special Branch Dave has found out some stuff on The Sacred Earth Militia. They're a pacifist environmentalist militia that seem to have morphed out of the Animal Rights Movement.

DIANE: A *pacifist militia*. What do you call that?

KEVIN: What? When two words in a phrase contradict.

DIANE: It's on the tip of my tongue.

GEOFF: Oxymoron.

DIANE: That's it!

KEVIN: Thank you Geoff.

GEOFF: Just doing my job. Facilitating excellence.

DIANE: Doesn't make any sense, "pacifist militia".

GEOFF: Neither did Led Zeppelin, but they did quite well.

DIANE: Did we catch him on video?

GEOFF: The kid's wearing a hoodie, and a balaclava, and army surplus fatigues.

KEVIN: Can't see his face?

GEOFF: No. But. Listen. Dave has run a check on Benjamin Orlando Shotter. He's a loner. Yeah. Lives on a canal boat. Alone. He's a loner who lives alone. Born in Brighton. And whadyerknow, The Sacred Earth Militia started in Brighton.

DIANE: You know, Special Branch haven't even spoken to me. I've had no advice, no offers of protection, I've not been interviewed –

GEOFF: – Yeah but –

DIANE: – Yeah but what?

KEVIN: Diane! Please!

GEOFF: You've got to be security cleared first.

DIANE: I don't need fucking security clearance, I'm the one being threatened!

KEVIN: Sorry Geoff.

GEOFF: I've worked hard on this. I wish I hadn't bothered.

(GEOFF turns to go, he's in a sulk.)

KEVIN: Geoff!

GEOFF: *(At the door.)* Tata.

(As he goes he turns the lamp off again, and gives an imperious glare to DIANE. He's gone.)

DIANE: There's your bloody IPCC report. I've used highlighter to identify statements that I consider to be politics.

KEVIN: *(Looking at it.)* It's all pink!

DIANE: Exactly.

KEVIN: "2.7 billion people could see greater water stress with global warming?" Why is that pink?

DIANE: You're cherry picking bad news. Why not tell us how many billions will have their water problems solved by climate change. Like most things to do with humans wet and warm is good.

KEVIN: Unless you're an Inuit.

DIANE: And that's a typo. The Himalayan glaciers will not have all melted by 2035, surely? I think you mean 2350.

KEVIN: OK. Thank you.

(KEVIN makes to go.)

DIANE: I'm scared Kevin.

KEVIN: About what?

DIANE: The fucking death threat!

(KEVIN sits reluctantly, dutifully.)

KEVIN: Alright. Good friend of mine, the UK archivist for The Grateful Dead, he works in research genetics – vivisection, hamsters. He uses hamsters because they breed like rabbits. He's had death threats. They painted his house red, and his car red, which was stupid actually because it was a red car. His wife couldn't handle it, she left him, but he was going to leave her anyway, not that she knew anything about that, but I did, because he'd told me, so he ended up saving himself about a hundred grand, and kept the house, which he certainly wasn't expecting –

DIANE: – what's your point?

KEVIN: They never actually tried to kill him. What's today? Wednesday. The day after the modular lecture. What was the subject yesterday?

DIANE: Paleoclimate proxy temperature reconstructions.

KEVIN: The Hockey Stick?

DIANE: It got a mention.

KEVIN: What did you say?

DIANE: I said that in the Roman Warming the Romans grew grapes as far north as Hadrian's wall, and in the Medieval Warming the Vikings colonised Greenland and grew corn. You know, all the stuff about natural climate cycles that you taught me. Before the Hockey Stick came along.

KEVIN: Doctor Popodopolos sat in on the lecture, at the back —

DIANE: — why?

KEVIN: He said that at one point instead of saying "climate change" you said "climate change, the artist formerly known as global warming".

DIANE: Doctor Popodopolos is an idiot.

KEVIN: Yes, I know.

DIANE: He's got a cuddly toy polar bear on his desk.

KEVIN: Did you communicate your scepticism of the Hockey Stick to the students?

DIANE: You're sceptical of the Hockey Stick!

KEVIN: Privately, yes, we all are, but every good thing that's happened in Paleo in the last ten years is because of the Hockey Stick.

DIANE: That's like getting in the society columns for murdering the Queen.

KEVIN: You can't go global warming sceptic on me! This is the faculty of Earth Sciences not the editorial office of the Spectator! All the evidence from the computer models suggests —

DIANE: — computer models are not evidence, they're just another hypothesis, or have you turned science on its head?! Computer modelling is what brought the global economy down. Computer modelling convinced you, thirty years ago that millions would die in a new ice age. I have your book. "Snowball Planet". Actually, you've never signed it.

(She stands and looks on her bookshelves.)

KEVIN: OK, unfortunately for me millions didn't die. We had one Commodore 64 between ten of us. I had twenty minutes on it every day when James Lovelock went for his mid-morning shit. That was then, and this is now, and now the vast majority of climate scientists have no doubt –

DIANE: – the vast majority of people on earth believe in God, and they're all wrong.

KEVIN: The "overwhelming consensus" of serious –

DIANE: – there was once an overwhelming consensus that the earth was the centre of the universe. Galileo –

KEVIN: – oh you're Galileo now are you!

DIANE: – Galileo didn't agree, got death threats, and no support from his peers.

KEVIN: OK. I'm shocked. I want you to put your hand up any time –

DIANE: – put my hand up?

KEVIN: Yeah. Put your hand up whenever you hear me make a statement that you do not believe to be true. One. Carbon dioxide is a greenhouse gas. *(Beat.)* You agree. Thank God for that.

DIANE: You can't treat me like this Kevin.

KEVIN: Two. Greenhouse gases absorb thermal radiation. *(Beat.)* Good. Going well. Three. Since the beginning of the industrial revolution we have increased the concentration of carbon dioxide in the atmosphere by thirty percent. *(Beat.)* Fine. Where are we?

DIANE: Four.

KEVIN: Four. Melting ice will reduce the earth's albedo so fewer of the sun's rays will be reflected back into space. As the oceans warm, they will expand, causing sea level rise. *(Beat.)*

DIANE: Five.

KEVIN: When the permafrost melts methane will be released.

DIANE: A much more potent greenhouse gas than CO_2.

KEVIN: Meaning what?

DIANE: Nothing, I was gilding your lily.

KEVIN: Yeah, well, it doesn't need it.

DIANE: I do one thing! One thing! I measure sea level!

KEVIN: In the Maldives!

DIANE: And it's not rising!

KEVIN: It is everywhere else! What's so special about the frigging Maldives!

DIANE: I've cracked it Kevin. For seventeen years I've been looking out to sea wondering why I can't record a sea level rise. I've been looking in the wrong place. The land is rising with the sea.

KEVIN: Isostasy?

DIANE: Oh you haven't forgotten. No, not isostasy. Low lying islands seem to be growing organically with sea level rise.

KEVIN: Coral?

DIANE: No! New sand, and sediment deposits are secured by ammophila grasses which protect them from wind and wave erosion. It's all in my paper.

(She gives him a copy of the Journal Energy, Ecology and Environment. KEVIN sits.)

You've sat down.

KEVIN: You little fucker. I told you not to publish.

DIANE: You told me not to send it to Toby, at Nature.

KEVIN: I meant don't send it to anyone. This rag is a sceptic's platform.

DIANE: It's a peer reviewed scientific journal.

KEVIN: Catalan will have a spotty youth reading everything published on sea level. You've handed Catalan on a plate to those cowboys at Hampshire University.

(KEVIN stands and closes the office door.)

DIANE: The man who introduced the open door policy has closed the door.

KEVIN: I'm going to have to give you a verbal warning, yes –

DIANE: – a what?

KEVIN: An informal verbal warning as part of the disciplinary procedure. Yes. For doing something I told you not to do, as your line manager.

DIANE: What's a line manager? We're not making Mars bars.

KEVIN: I'll get you a written copy of this verbal warning as soon as I can.

DIANE: So it's not a verbal warning it's a written warning?

KEVIN: I think I've got to do you a letter which will act as a record of the verbal warning.

DIANE: But that'll make it a written warning.

KEVIN: Oh hells bells! I don't know. Just hang on.

(He picks up the phone and dials a three digit internal number.)

KEVIN: *(On the phone.)* Miss Tickell? … it's me… Professor Maloney… yes, I've had to issue Doctor Cassell with a verbal warning… ok, well I'm sorry, I forgot…

(To Diane.) You've got the right to a union rep with you apparently. Do you want one?

DIANE: Fuck off.

KEVIN: *(On the phone.)* I don't think she wants one. Do I need to give her a written record of the verbal warning, warning?…no, ok, I just make a note for myself in my own records…and that can be in writing can it? …of course. Thank you.

(He puts the phone down.)

Right! You can't have it in writing, that would make it a written warning. The verbal warning is in verbal only.

DIANE: But I want it in writing!

KEVIN: A written warning is stage two.

DIANE: Let's go straight to stage two then!

KEVIN: But stage two is really serious!

DIANE: And stage one is just a bit of a laugh?!

KEVIN: Look! You've had the verbal, and that's all you're fucking getting!

DIANE: I want a written warning! It can't be more serious than a death threat.

(She begins to cry. KEVIN is marooned.)

KEVIN: Oh hell's bells D.

DIANE: Don't call me D! And I'm not crying.

KEVIN: Look –

DIANE: – *(To herself.)* oh God, stop it! Stop it! I never cry. Never, ever.

KEVIN: No, no, it's er…it's good to cry.

DIANE: No it's not. It's so weak. Stop it woman! Stop it. I promised myself I would not ever cry about this fucking death threat!

(A knock at the door. DIANE is still crying.)

KEVIN: Shit. There's someone at the door.

DIANE: Let them in.

KEVIN: But you're still crying.

DIANE: *(Crying.)* I'm not crying! I don't know what this is. Let them in. I'll stop if it's a stranger.

(KEVIN opens the door, slightly reluctantly. DIANE is still crying. PHOEBE comes in.)

KEVIN: Ah! Phoebe, hello.

PHOEBE: – is she crying?

DIANE: No!

PHOEBE: What have you said to my mum?

DIANE: – he's given me a verbal warning.

PHOEBE: Why have you given her a verbal warning? My mum's brilliant. I'll give you a verbal warning – fuck off!

(KEVIN starts to back out. He's gone. PHOEBE puts an arm round DIANE. She's still crying.)

PHOEBE: You had a death threat, didn't cry once, you get a verbal warning and you go all Gwyneth Paltrow on me. What does this verbal warning say, where is it? I want to read it.

DIANE: It's verbal. It's not written down.

PHOEBE: This place is weird.

(Knock at the door. PHOEBE goes to the door.)

PHOEBE: Who is it?

BEN: *(Off.)* Ben Shotter. First year PaleoGeophysics.

PHOEBE: It's the cute boy mum! Can we let him in. Please!

(DIANE nods. PHOEBE opens the door.)

Hi Ben.

BEN: Oh. Yeah. It's you. Safe.

DIANE: What is it Ben?

BEN: Got a tutorial.

PHOEBE: She's been crying.

DIANE: Urgh! Sit down.

PHOEBE: Sit down Ben.

(BEN sits on one of the tutorial chairs.)

BEN: *(To Phoebe.)* I sent you a friend request on Facebook. Archimedes.

PHOEBE: Oh that was you was it?

BEN: Yeah, that oil painting of Archimedes is like my Facebook icon, yeah?

PHOEBE: Oh. I thought that was what you looked like.

(Beat.) How did you find me on Facebook?

BEN: Chill man, I did a search, alright, on your name.

PHOEBE: You don't know my name. It's not the same as hers.

DIANE: Observe the world, find a variable which when doubled does not have a doubling effect.

BEN: Yeah. So I went out the other day, yeah, on a bike ride, and I observed the real world yeah and I've got this idea, kinda like an hypothesis.

PHOEBE: Like a young attractive Archimedes on a bike might have.

BEN: Yeah!

DIANE: Phoebe! This is work. I'll be ten minutes.

PHOEBE: I understand what's going on. She's fucking with your head. Three years of her and you'll be working for Exxon Mobil. Be strong Archimedes.

(PHOEBE leaves.)

BEN: I was cycling past this chicken farm, yeah, and there was this like fence made of wire mesh, and then beyond that a second fence made of like the same gauge wire –

DIANE: – the same size holes?

BEN: Yeah! Pointless! If a chicken is small enough to get through the first fence, it's gonna get through the second fence an'all, innit.

(Beat.)

DIANE: And from this observation you have formed an hypothesis about the relationship between CO_2 and temperature?

BEN: Yeah. I've called it the thermal chicken theory. The first bit of CO_2 –

DIANE: – "the first bit?"

BEN: The first 280 parts per million CO_2 is the first fence. Shit, I should've started with the chickens. The sun, yeah, fires thermal chickens at the earth. The chickens bounce and start heading back into space but get trapped by the first fence –

DIANE: – the pre-industrial carbon dioxide.

BEN: – yeah, that first fence traps all of the thermal chickens in the wavelength band 14 to 16.5 microns. The second fence –

DIANE: – the next 100 parts per million anthropogenic CO_2?

BEN: – yeah, has nothing to do, all the work's been done.

DIANE: This is a saturation theory of CO_2. You're challenging the accepted logarithmic relationship between CO_2 and temperature. You're saying that anthropogenic CO_2 does not cause warming. A sceptic's fantasy.

BEN: Look, I just saw these two stupid fences round a chicken farm.

DIANE: It's a bit mad, but OK. How are you going to test it?

BEN: Dunno. Fun innit. Science. Yeah.

DIANE: I think so, yes. You have an hypothesis, now you need an experimental design.

BEN: I'd need a scale model of the earth, with a cryoshroud –

DIANE: – write it down. Next week. How's the coal cars assignment?

BEN: You only gave me that to piss me off. To attack my belief system.

DIANE: I'm trying to teach the importance of scepticism.

BEN: The shield of science, and the sword of scepticism.

DIANE: OK we'll move on. This paper is a proxy temperature reconstruction using tree ring data. Kieron McKay, University of Hampshire. We're going to peer review it.

BEN: It's in Nature, it's already been peer reviewed.

DIANE: Yeah, by his best friend.

BEN: But if this guy's been all the way to China –

DIANE: – I know Kieron McKay, he wouldn't stray five hundred yards from a subsidised canteen. Our job is to try and replicate his results. That is how science moves forward. But Kieron McKay is destroying the thing I hold most dear, that process. He's refused to release his data. I've taken out a Freedom of Information Request.

BEN: This don't sound like science. You have an agenda man!

DIANE: Of which I'm aware.

BEN: I'm up for it.

(He stands, makes to leave.)

DIANE: I heard you moved off campus.

BEN: Had to yeah, they turned the heating on.

DIANE: How's the new place?

BEN: It's a boat on the River Oose. But British Waterways are pressuring me, yeah. I don't have a license. I'm stressed man, I don't know what to do.

DIANE: You could get a license.

BEN: Yeah, that's a good idea.

DIANE: What is it, a barge?

BEN: A narrow boat.

DIANE: Great. What's it like?

BEN: Alright. Bit narrow.

(He closes the door.)

End of Scene.

SCENE TWO

(The Newsnight studio.)

PAXMAN: Mark Urban from Stonehenge. The President of the Maldives recently held a cabinet meeting under water.

(Photo of President Nasheed and cabinet in wet suits under water.)

Rising sea level, he claims, is a threat to his islands. So, are we in the West to blame, and should we be made to pay? We're joined now by Ahmed Waheed, the Maldives High Commissioner to London, and Doctor Diane Cassell from the Earth Sciences Faculty of YUIST. High Commissioner, if this is a publicity stunt, what's the message?

WAHEED: We are the lowest lying nation on earth. Our President is saying "Western industry, western pollution, your lifestyles" –

DIANE: – like flying to the Maldives for a holiday –

PAXMAN: – hang on!

WAHEED: – you in the West are slowly killing us.

PAXMAN: Doctor Cassell, you don't buy this do you?

DIANE: I've been measuring Maldives sea level for nearly twenty years, it's not rising. The President can tell his people to relax and enjoy their island paradise.

PAXMAN: High Commissioner, I'm presuming you have scientific evidence to support your fears?

WAHEED: Greenpeace, the World Wildlife Fund, environment NGOs, they all say –

DIANE: – they're not scientists, they're advocacy groups –

WAHEED: – the IPCC –

DIANE: – a UN committee with a political agenda –

PAXMAN: – Doctor Cassell, please. High Commissioner –

WAHEED: The IPCC is reporting an annual sea level rise of 2.3 millimetres.

PAXMAN: 2.3 millimetres? I've got kidney stones bigger than that.

WAHEED: We have not one island higher than two metres above sea level.

PAXMAN: This is the point isn't it, even these tiny annual rises are the death knell to low lying nations.

DIANE: The IPCC is a political body and should be ignored.

PAXMAN: But presumably this 2.3 millimetre rise was measured and observed by one of your colleagues.

DIANE: The researcher has used a single tide gauge in Hong Kong harbour, a port built on shale sediment which is prone to compaction.

PAXMAN: You're saying he's not measuring sea level rise, he's measuring how much the pier he's nailed his tide gauge to is sinking?

DIANE: You'd make a good climate scientist Jeremy. You have a laser eye for the truth and a natural grumpy scepticism.

PAXMAN: Thank you, I think. And thirty years in the BBC means I know a bit about chaos. Are you conning us High Commissioner?

WAHEED: All the global warming deniers live in the West. We did not cause the problem, you did, so the bill must land on your mat.

PAXMAN: Doctor Cassell, are you a global warming *denier*?

DIANE: There is no evidence that CO_2 is the cause of twentieth-century warming.

PAXMAN: You're pretty much alone in this belief aren't you.

DIANE: It's not a belief. I'm a scientist, I don't "believe" in anything.

PAXMAN: Is it your assessment then that the IPCC are being alarmist?

DIANE: The real global warming disaster is that a small cohort of hippies who went into climate science because they could get paid for spending all day on the beach smoking joints have suddenly become the most powerful people in the world.

PAXMAN: *(Laughing.)* With that trenchant assessment of your colleagues, we'll have to leave it there. Like mankind, we've run out of time, or maybe not. Thank you both.

(To different camera.) Sea levels may be rising, but bee levels are falling. The global population of bees –

To black.

End of Scene.

Act Three

SCENE ONE

(December. Heavy snow is falling. BEN has just come in and is standing, very well wrapped up in jumpers and scarves. His clothes are matted with snow.)

BEN: I've heard, that the other lecturers have stopped talking to you.

DIANE: I'm about as welcome in this building as Abu Hamza at a hook-a-duck stall.

BEN: That's racist. No. Disablist. Semantic specificity.

DIANE: You're learning.

(He shuts the door.)

BEN: Been thinking about killing myself.

DIANE: This is in my diary as a tutorial to discuss clouds. Have you seen the student counsellor?

BEN: I can't. She drives an Alfa Romeo. I thought you might have been trained in, like, I dunno, active listening skills?

(He sits.)

DIANE: *(Picks up his essay.)* Your essay… doesn't adequately –

BEN: – you don't want to talk about my suicide attempt?

DIANE: No. I was hoping for an acknowledgment of the complexity of climate dynamics. Einstein said "before I die I hope someone will explain quantum physics to me, after I die, I hope God will explain turbulence".

BEN: Einstein was a wanker. He cheated on his wife.

DIANE: Did you know his wife?

BEN: No.

DIANE: Don't judge him then.

BEN: That's what fascinates me about climate man. That kind of endless infinity dynamism which almost by definition cannot be modelled, or written about cogently, 'cause it's what it is, it is like totally random man, it is…ha! It's too difficult, there's just too many fucking factors man, it's unpredictable, beyond prediction, it's massive, massive, it's a beast, I mean, if you could do it, you couldn't do it, you'd get it wrong, it's proper harsh, like endless turbulence, it's infinity, it's chaos.

DIANE: That's what I was looking for in the essay. Climate is stochastic.

BEN: What does stochastic mean?

DIANE: "Like totally random man".

BEN: Don't take the piss out of someone who is suicidal. Ridicule can have no part in student centred learning.

(BEN stands and from his pocket he takes a Stanley knife – the retracting blade type.)

DIANE: What's that Ben?

BEN: It's a Stanley knife. Six ninety nine, B and Q.

DIANE: What are you going to do with it?

BEN: Hobby stuff?

(He rolls his sleeve up to reveal his left wrist.)

DIANE: Do you always slash your wrists in front of people?

BEN: What it is yeah, I get these waves of happiness man, standing in a queue, anywhere, this wave of joy just hits me. And it's a shock, and it pisses me off, 'cause I'm not happy, so it's an invasion really, yeah? I feel this pressure, the future, like weighing down on me, and I'm stressed again, and that's alright, it's shit, yeah, but that's what I'm used to, feel comfortable with that. Do you get them? Like funny waves of happiness. Inexplicable.

DIANE: Yes.

BEN: Why is it that everything that humans touch turns to shit?

DIANE: Beavers don't hate themselves because they gnaw down trees.

BEN: I've joined Vehement. You can join online. D'ya know them?

DIANE: No.

BEN: Stands for Voluntary Human Exctinction Movement. We believe that the biosphere, earth, would be better off without humans. We're working towards removing human life from earth by non-reproduction.

DIANE: I'll join. I can't do Tuesdays.

BEN: Taking the piss again. I don't eat you know. All food has to travel, so I don't eat, except locally grown vegetables. And if I do eat I fart, that's methane, methane is a greenhouse gas. That's why I eat garlic. There's compounds in garlic, yeah, that kill off the methane. And when I breathe, yeah, I breathe in like half a percent of carbon dioxide, and when I breathe out, yeah, 'cause I've consumed oxygen from the air five percent of my emissions –

DIANE: – your *emissions?*

BEN: – yeah, my out breath is like a massive five percent carbon dioxide.

DIANE: To get your carbon footprint down to nothing, you'd have to kill yourself, and not be cremated.

BEN: Yeah.

DIANE: This aggression towards yourself, do you ever turn that on others. Car drivers for example?

BEN: The perfect death for me would be to blow myself up on Top Gear.

DIANE: Have you ever physically attacked anyone?

BEN: Yeah, when I was eighteen. My dad. I caught him watching porn. I hit him on the head with one of them orange casserole dishes.

DIANE: Le Creuset?

BEN: Yeah.

DIANE: They're really heavy.

BEN: And it was hot.

DIANE: It must've hurt him.

BEN: Put it this way, he stopped wanking.

DIANE: It's perfectly normal for a boy to hate his dad. You should start to see your life as a –

BEN: – "should" – that's didactic. My therapist never uses the "should" word.

DIANE: Have you had a lot of therapy?

BEN: Yeah.

DIANE: How am I doing?

BEN: You're crap. You haven't even worked out that I hate myself 'cause I killed my mother in childbirth.

DIANE: I thought that was so obvious it wasn't worth saying. Every man and woman that has ever been born on this earth has eaten, and kept themselves warm.

BEN: Somthing terrible has happened. Bust this. My dad has gone green. Like bare mad green. He's scrapped the Volvo, bought solar panels, started cycling. And my brain is like totally fing!

DIANE: You're suffering from what psychologists call cognitive dissonance. That doesn't help does it?

BEN: No.

DIANE: If you like Gary Glitter, and hate child porn, and then one day it's in the news that Gary is into child porn, you

will suffer cognitive dissonance. To regain balance you
must decide that you no longer like Gary Glitter.

BEN: Or… you could get into child porn.

DIANE: Yes! That would give you balance. This is an
opportunity for you to love your dad.

BEN: I hate the bastard.

DIANE: OK. But you have to find balance somehow.

BEN: I think I could hate like unquestioning greens, who don't
know anything about Earth Sciences but who just buy stuff
'cause they're gullible or do stuff 'cause they're credulous,
or just 'cause they think it's cool.

DIANE: People like your dad. So that's achieving balance by
carrying on hating your dad?

BEN: Yeah.

DIANE: OK then. Can we do some work now? Kieron McKay
has rejected my Freedom of Information Request.

BEN: Hampshire University?

DIANE: Yes. There's something dodgy going on. And
that excites me and should excite you, since it's your
assignment.

BEN: Is that your best shot? To get my mind off this?

DIANE: I'm not a therapist. I'm a fossil basher. You're lucky
I'm not using a hammer.

(BEN runs the knife along the skin. A little blood shows.)

Ben! Please, just, please don't do that.

(Beat.) Phoebe asked after you. I think she likes you.

BEN: Can I come for Christmas?

DIANE: No.

BEN: What do you do at Christmas?

DIANE: My brother drives my mother over for Christmas dinner. On Boxing Day my mother makes a turkey bolognese Irish hot pot lasagne. We eat it, Phoebe throws it up, and my brother takes my mother home. Phoebe and I go for a walk over the hills to this Medieval abandoned village. The ruins of a church, manor house, you know, it's fun.

BEN: Can I come for the walk?

DIANE: Are you going to be alone on the boat?

BEN: Yeah.

DIANE: I'll ask Phoebe.

BEN: No way man! Don't tell her!

DIANE: You like Phoebe?

BEN: She's mint, yeah.

DIANE: Just turn up then. After lunch.

BEN: I know, with an essay!? No. That's crap.

DIANE: It's a village off the A166, on the way to Bridlington. Fimber.

BEN: *(Writing.)* Fimber? I'll Google Earth it.

DIANE: Go a mile through the village, pond on your left. Manor Barns.

BEN: A converted barn?

DIANE: Yeah.

BEN: Cool! Er… Merry Christmas.

DIANE: Keep warm. Burn something you're allowed to burn.

(BEN is gone. The door is left open. DIANE is thoughtful. KEVIN sticks his head round.)

KEVIN: Are you…?

DIANE: Yes.

KEVIN: I didn't think you'd make it in.

DIANE: I had a morning of tutorials.

KEVIN: You don't still do tutorials do you?

DIANE: Yes.

KEVIN: They're not cost effective. The radio said the Wolds were white over.

DIANE: They are. How did you get in?

KEVIN: Mrs Nextdoor gave me a lift in her 4x4.

DIANE: She's forgiven you for running over her cat?

KEVIN: Yes. Fascinating woman. She used to be in the IRA. Yeah. Properly worked for them as a quartermaster.

DIANE: What does she do now?

KEVIN: She's the ski wear buyer at Millets. Did you drive?

DIANE: Phoebe was brilliant. She put her boots on, and walked out into the blizzard. Ten minutes later she pulled up the drive on a tractor, hitched a rope to the Jag, and towed me down to the main road, which was gritted. She crushed my favourite rose in the operation.

KEVIN: Shame.

DIANE: It was a wild white rose, a cutting I took from a hedge.

KEVIN: I'm sorry.

DIANE: Don't be sorry Kevin. It was a plant.

(KEVIN sits down.)

Oh dear. You've sat down.

KEVIN: Miss Tickell from Human Resources will be joining us in a minute.

DIANE: Frau Tickell?

KEVIN: I've arranged for Doctor Popodopolos to take over all your teaching for the rest of the term.

DIANE: Fuck off.

KEVIN: I'm the Professor here! I'm unfuckoffable.

DIANE: I've had sex with you. In a tent. I can tell you to fuck off whenever I like!

KEVIN: Hells bells! What made you think that you could be fucking interviewed on fucking Paxo, representing my fucking Earth Sciences Faculty of York University Institute of Science and fucking Technology and not ask for permission from either me, or the Vice fucking Chancellor?!

DIANE: Because the fucking BBC needed a fucking sea level expert. It was either me or Doctor Popofuckingdopolos.

(There is a knock at the door. DIANE opens the door to MISS TICKELL.)

I know you. You're one of the human resources of Human Resources.

TICKELL: Catherine Tickell.

DIANE: Guten morgen. What's going on Kevin?

KEVIN: We're going to have to suspend you.

TICKELL: You have the right to be accompanied by a union official or colleague.

DIANE: Alright. I'll go and find my union official. Ein Augenblick, bitte!

(DIANE exits, closing the door. TICKELL and KEVIN sit.)

TICKELL: Why is she speaking German?

KEVIN: I don't know. Insane! She home educated her daughter, six years. That's not normal is it. No-one's good enough to teach her precious Phoebe. Poor kid. Made her an anorexic.

TICKELL: I've got a tip for these sort of situations, say as little as possible, think before you speak, bite your tongue, count to ten.

KEVIN: I want her out of my building.

TICKELL: When do Catalan visit?

KEVIN: January.

TICKELL: Who's the union rep in Earth Sciences?

KEVIN: Doctor Popodopolos.

TICKELL: Oh Christ.

(Re-enter DIANE carrying DOCTOR POPODOPOLOS's cuddly toy polar bear. DIANE sits behind her desk and plonks the polar bear on the desk, holding it, moving it so it seems to look around the room taking in the scene.)

DIANE: This is my shop steward, Maureen. Kevin. Say hello to Maureen.

KEVIN: Nice to meet you Maureen.

DIANE: *(As MAUREEN.)* Hellooo!

Miss Tickle?

TICKELL: Tickell.

DIANE: Sorry. Say hello to Maureen.

(TICKELL is biting her tongue and counting to ten.)

TICKELL: Hello.

DIANE: Maureen.

TICKELL: Hello Maureen.

DIANE: *(As MAUREEN.)* Hellooo!

Lovely! Now, how can I help?

KEVIN: I'm sorry Diane –

TICKELL: – no. We are progressing from your verbal warning to stage three, suspension, on the grounds of mental capacity.

DIANE: Surely, "mental incapacity"? Or "lack of" mental capacity?

TICKELL: In employment law it's called mental capacity.

DIANE: I bet you're good fun at parties.

TICKELL: It is outside your contractual terms to give a
media interview as an employee of the university without
prior clearance from your line manager, and the Vice
Chancellor. Additionally, the sceptical position you have
taken on climate change damages the image of Professor
Maloney's Climate Change Research Unit, which threatens
its ability to raise industry funding in the market place.
Consequently we require that you go for an assessment of
your mental capacity to fulfil your contract.

DIANE: You're sacking me because you think I'm mad?

TICKELL: This is not dismissal, this is suspension on the
grounds of mental capacity pending medical assessment.
Do you have any questions?

DIANE: I do, yes. Only one. What happened to the beautiful
boy I fell in love with in a tent overlooking Isafjord?

(Silence.)

TICKELL: If you're making an unlawful sexual harrassment
accusation against –

KEVIN: – it's alright.

DIANE: He began his seduction by teaching me how to gut a
cod. Stick your thumb and index finger in the fish's eyes,
the eyes will pop out, but, hell's bells, don't cry for me
Argentina, the fish is dead. Find the gateway of bones
below the gills and run the knife quickly south dragging
the guts out with your trailing thumb. Wash the fish in the
fjord, triple wrap in foil and place in the embers. Whilst
it's cooking, create a map sized Rizla, spread evenly with
tobacco from two broken cigarettes, and dress with the
crumblings from a lump of Lebanese. Lick the Rizla along
its length, and look the girl in the eye. She will blush. Tell
her your heroes. Robert Johnson – King of the Delta Blues
singers, Charles II, Henry Miller, Rosa Parks – why Rosa

Parks and not Martin Luther King? Because her motivation was pure, not political. She was on a bus, tired, and she wanted to sit down. Your enemies were hilarious. Mother Theresa of Calcutta – pure evil?! Gandhi – a cretin!? The clergy of all religions. On science, brilliant, but frightened. The enlightenment project would never be secure because of the ubiquitous human need to be crushed under the wheels of the supernatural. And then a hand found its way under my jumper and cupped my left breast. I welcomed it. I was in love. That was a tutorial, Kevin. Not cost effective obviously, but inspirational. What happened to you? *(Beat.)* I've finished. You can sack me now.

TICKELL: You will get a letter outlining your rights and your responsibilities. We require you to leave the campus immediately.

DIANE: Can I confer with my colleague?

TICKELL: Er…yes.

(DIANE whispers into the polar bear's ear. The polar bear whispers back into DIANE's ear.)

DIANE: Maureen says that in the twenty seven years she's worked in industrial relations she's never met a bigger pair of cunts.

To black.

Interval.

Act Four

SCENE ONE

(Boxing Day afternoon. Not yet dark. DIANE's kitchen in the country. Main entrance door up stage centre, which is a stable door design ie: top half opens independently. Open stairs. The back wall has a big picture window, the old barn entrance, through which we see that although it is not snowing now, snow has fallen and drifted. PHOEBE and DIANE sit at the table staring at a Scrabble board. A laptop is plugged in and set beside PHOEBE.)

PHOEBE: Why did you invite that *fucking insane* Mrs Boston over for Christmas dinner yesterday?

DIANE: Mrs Boston is my mother.

PHOEBE: Why doesn't she like Polish people?

DIANE: Because they're doing the kind of jobs she'd like to be doing, for the kind of money she'd like to be earning.

PHOEBE: I lay in bed last night listening to you two down here. I heard every word of her white supremacist manifesto.

DIANE: You still need to thank her for your present.

PHOEBE: She bought me the box set Delia Smith.

DIANE: I suggested knee pads.

PHOEBE: Knee pads?

DIANE: For all the puking up you do.

PHOEBE: Bitch. I need alcohol.

DIANE: We have contracted with Maeve not to drink until it's dark.

PHOEBE: Uurgh! I bet Boxing Day on a London sink estate isn't this boring.

DIANE: What would you be doing Phoebe?

PHOEBE: I'd deal some skunk; stick fireworks through a paedophile's letter box; organise a dog fight in a lock up; watch some porn; buy a gun; get drunk; Super Glue a tortoise to the railway lines; bomb some amphetamine; go home and have sex with my step dad. Yes! What a fucking brilliant Christmas! But no, I'm middle class, so I play Scrabble.

(PHOEBE lays four tiles to make LIONPERM. DIANE frowns.)

DIANE: Lionperm?

PHOEBE: Ya.

DIANE: What's a lionperm?

PHOEBE: A hair do. Makes you look a bit like a lion.

DIANE: I challenge.

(PHOEBE opens the dictionary as if to look for lionperm.)

PHOEBE: Lingerie. Lion. Lioness. *Lionperm.* A hairstyle originating in South Shields remarkable for the mane-like ridge of hair matted with blood and excrement. Triple word. Thirty nine.

DIANE: Take your tiles back.

PHOEBE: No! I refuse to conform to the rules of this quasi-educational, fascist mind fuck, wank fest.

(DIANE sighs, looks at her watch, and then out the window. Starts recycling.)

DIANE: If I put bones in the organic waste will I be arrested?

PHOEBE: Why have we not gone on our walk to Wharram Percy?!

DIANE: The snow on the tops is drifting. It's getting dark. It's dangerous. We might die.

PHOEBE: I want to die. I wish your mother had aborted you. And I wish you'd aborted me. I'm never gonna have kids.

DIANE: We can't recycle the dead.

PHOEBE: This planet cannot sustain an ever growing population.

DIANE: Alright! We need to give Len his Christmas presents, and I need half a dozen eggs.

PHOEBE: Anything to get out of this place. Len's is twenty yards. That's not a Boxing Day walk.

(PHOEBE puts her coat and wellies on. Picks up LEN's present – a wrapped bottle of whisky.)

DIANE: If Len says come in for a cup of tea, I'm not going in, he's filthy.

PHOEBE: Eighty six-year-old farmers who live on their own don't hoover.

(DIANE puts her coat and wellies on. She picks up a present, a small wrapped block.)

PHOEBE: Whisky. You?

DIANE: Soap.

PHOEBE: Fascist. I hate you.

DIANE: The reasons why we hate each other are many and complex.

PHOEBE: No they're not. I'm an active member of Greenpeace and you're a gas guzzling planet rapist.

(They leave. DIANE makes a point of locking the door.)

(Off.) Why are you locking the door?!

DIANE: *(Off.)* Because I'm mad and I keep imagining I've had death threats.

(We see them walk off in the direction of the road. Silence. Then the landline phone rings and rings, then off. Someone in ski mask and fatigues approaches the house, looks in the window. He unlocks the door with keys and enters. He closes the door behind him. He locks the door. He has a cursory look around. He takes off his ski mask.

It is GEOFF. He is cold. He seeks out warmth. Then he takes his mobile phone out and presses a preset.)

GEOFF: *(On phone.)* It's me, Geoff. I'm in the house...where the fuck are you?...I told you not to use the van, chip fat coagulates in these temperatures. On a mission it's important to have total confidence in your equipment... OK ignore me, I mean, I was only in the Marines...listen Tara, change of plan, I'm gonna hide indoors, upstairs... 'cause it's fucking freezing in the barn!... park west of the pond and text me, when you get here...tarra.

(GEOFF is off the phone. He goes in the fridge, finds something to eat, eats it. He takes all the knives from a knife block, wraps them in a tea towel and puts them inside his jacket. He is distracted by the Scrabble board, takes one look, looks away moves on, stops himself, looks back at it again. Picks up the dictionary, starts to check LIONPERM. The sound of PHOEBE's voice in the garden.)

PHOEBE: *(Off.)* That is just so rude!

DIANE: *(Off.)* I can't stand the smell.

PHOEBE: *(Off.)* That's what farmers smell like.

DIANE: *(Off.)* I'm not disputing that.

(Unlocking the door.)

GEOFF: Oh shit!

(GEOFF crouches and runs for the stairs. He disappears upstairs as DIANE is unlocking the door. DIANE and PHOEBE come in. DIANE is carrying a box of eggs.)

PHOEBE: Why can't we go on our proper walk? You're punishing me for last night.

DIANE: I will punish you for last night when I can think of something appropriately elegant.

PHOEBE: You deserved to be punched.

DIANE: You have contracted with Maeve to stop punching me.

PHOEBE: No! I have a contract with Maeve to *try* to stop punching you. Semantic specificity. You – *try* to drop this wooden spoon.

(She gives DIANE a wooden spoon. DIANE lifts it up and drops it.)

PHOEBE: I didn't ask you to drop it, I asked you to *try* and drop it.

DIANE: You hurt me. I'm your mother.

PHOEBE: That's why I hurt you. When I punch you it is me *trying* to stop punching you. This is how you *try* to drop a spoon.

(PHOEBE holds the wooden spoon up and tries to drop it, holding on to it all the while. She becomes distressed with the effort, breathing hard, crying.)

DIANE: Phoebs! Stop it! OK, I get it! Stop it!

(PHOEBE throws the spoon away. She is now distraught. DIANE comforts her. Sound of a car pulling into the drive. A mobile phone rings – Megadeth ringtone.)

DIANE: What the fuck?!

PHOEBE: Megadeth. That's your mobile.

DIANE: You changed my ringtone again?

(DIANE locates the phone and answers after first looking at the display.)

DIANE: Kevin?

(On phone.) What do you want? …we're having a traditional Christmas, almost Dickensian in its various extremes of suffering…you're where?…oh my God…OK.

(Off the phone.)

PHOEBE: What's he want?

DIANE: He's parked in the drive.

(PHOEBE looks out the window. Sound of car door slamming.)

PHOEBE: He sacked you mum!

(There is a knock. PHOEBE opens only the top half of the stable style door. This reveals KEVIN, holding a climbing rose, unwrapped.)

PHOEBE: Fuck off!

KEVIN: Merry Christmas!

(PHOEBE closes the door. DIANE approaches the door, opens it.)

DIANE: Is it cold out there?

KEVIN: Severe Negative Arctic Oscillation, combined with an Extreme Negative North Atlantic Oscillation and a strong La Nina are blocking any moderation from the Gulf Stream.

DIANE: You're saying it's too cold to snow?

KEVIN: This is for you. I got it today. Take it, please!

(He hands in the climbing rose. DIANE takes it and puts it on the table. It looks pathetic.)

PHOEBE: What is it? A board game?

KEVIN: No. It's a climbing rose. Rambling Rector. It's won awards.

DIANE: Not this one surely?

KEVIN: No, you know, the breed. Best climbing rose.

DIANE: What are the judges looking for? Speed?

PHOEBE: Where did you steal it from?

KEVIN: You said Phoebe had accidentally run over your favourite climbing rose.

PHOEBE: I don't do anything accidentally.

KEVIN: It's from that garden centre just this side of Flamborough Head.

DIANE: You went to Flamborough Head on your own? On Boxing Day?

KEVIN: No. I went to the garden centre just this side of Flamborough Head.

DIANE: On your own, on Boxing Day?

KEVIN: Sabina's been having an affair. She's left me.

DIANE: At Christmas?

PHOEBE: I'm in an episode of EastEnders!

(DIANE opens the door and lets KEVIN in. Closes the door after him.)

KEVIN: Thank you.

PHOEBE: *(To DIANE.)* You're weak! Have you had sex with him?

DIANE: Once.

PHOEBE: Why only once? Is he rubbish?

KEVIN: She means *once* as in once upon a time.

PHOEBE: Would you like a glass of red wine?

KEVIN: Thank you, but I'm driving, so I can only have the one.

DIANE: And would you like that one now?

KEVIN: Yes please.

PHOEBE: Large or small?

KEVIN: Large please.

(PHOEBE gets herself a glass of red. And pours one for KEVIN.)

DIANE: Very clever.

PHOEBE: *(Drinking.)* It's genetic.

KEVIN: You've seen the papers, obviously.

DIANE: I told you about that typo.

KEVIN: They're calling it Glaciergate.

DIANE: Why didn't you get it proofed properly?

PHOEBE: Transparency!

DIANE: Kevin is like a rash across all the papers. If you read them, you'd know. They're all going crazy about a typo, which I spotted three months ago, in his IPCC chapter which says that the Himalayan glaciers will all have melted by 2035.

PHOEBE: Sounds reasonable to me.

DIANE: That's because you *want* them to melt.

KEVIN: *(To PHOEBE.)* The date is about three hundred years wrong.

DIANE: 2035. 2350. I knew you weren't listening to me, I –

KEVIN: – it wasn't a typo.

(KEVIN sits.)

I knew it wasn't a typo. I put it in deliberately. I got the date from a WWF document.

DIANE: Oh my God! Oh fuck! You put some made up stuff from an activist in the IPCC report. When this gets out they're gonna crucify you. What were you doing?

KEVIN: The people in the foothills, I've been there, I know them, they're really really beautiful people when you get used to them, they depend on the glaciers, the melt waters. They need action now, not in three hundred years' time.

PHOEBE: I don't think you've done anything wrong.

DIANE: Oh he has, and he knows he has!

KEVIN: You don't understand D!

DIANE: Don't call me D!

KEVIN: You don't have to talk to politicians. I do, it's impossible, they're all so –

DIANE: – thick?

PHOEBE: Liars yes, but thick?

DIANE: If Frankenstein went into the House of Commons, chopped them all up, he wouldn't be able to build one single decent scientist.

KEVIN: If I asked you for a prediction of sea level rise in a hundred years' time. What would you say?

DIANE: Ten centimeters plus or minus fifteen.

KEVIN: Yes! Doubt! That's no bloody use to a politician. They need me to say with absolute certainty that Edinburgh castle is gonna be six foot under on New Year's Eve 2050.

DIANE: Nothing changes unless everyone is shit scared.

(KEVIN takes a drink, empties his glass.)

PHOEBE: Your glass is empty. And you can only have one because you're driving.

KEVIN: I'll be alright, it's an automatic.

DIANE: It may well be an automatic Kevin, but you still have to be there.

(PHOEBE pours him another glass.)

KEVIN: Ta. How are you?

PHOEBE: You sacked her! And then you come here, to our home, on Boxing Day, drink our cheapest Chianti, and refuse to eat our Turkish Delights.

KEVIN: You haven't offered me a Turkish Delight.

PHOEBE: Do you want one?

KEVIN: No thanks.

PHOEBE: Have you been reading her column in the Daily Telegraph?

KEVIN: Yes. Very provocative. Your tree, in the Maldives; sea levels not rising; Al Gore buys beach house.

DIANE: They've offered me a regular column.

PHOEBE: Can you tell her that writing for the Telegraph is not a victimless crime.

DIANE: They want a hard scientist to go head to head with George Monbiot.

PHOEBE: Fight! Fight! Fight! Fight! Fight! Fight! Fight! Fight! Fight! Fight!

KEVIN: Are you going to take it?

DIANE: I don't want to be the leader of the British sceptics.

KEVIN: Pin-up girl surely.

DIANE: I'm a sceptic because I have no choice, the science isn't good enough. But *they* have chosen to be sceptics. No amount of quality science will persuade them. They would sooner eat the family labrador.

KEVIN: I've eaten dog.

PHOEBE: Korea?

KEVIN: Birmingham.

DIANE: Why did you come here today Kevin?

PHOEBE: It's obvious. He was going to throw himself off Flamborough Head because of this Himalayan thing, because his wife has left him, and because Christmas is always a bit shit.

KEVIN: I thought that looking at the ocean, might give me some perspective, which it did. Which is why I bought you a rose. I'm not suicidal.

(He finishes his second glass.)

PHOEBE: You're definitely alcoholic.

(There is a knock at the door.)

I knew you were expecting someone!

(BEN appears at the window.)

Shit! It's that cute student. Mum! And I look like a yak!

(PHOEBE puts a hat on.)

KEVIN: What's a yak? Is that like a goth?

DIANE: No. A yak is a Tibetan cow.

(DIANE opens the door. He has cycled. His left wrist is bandaged.)

Hello Ben!

BEN: Have you got wifi?

DIANE: We do. You cycled? In this.

BEN: *(Keen.)* Hi.

PHOEBE: *(Dismissive.)* Hi.

DIANE: You know Professor Maloney, Kevin.

KEVIN: Whappen?!

BEN: What?

KEVIN: Hi.

BEN: Hi.

DIANE: Sit here Ben. Get warm. Would you like a drink?

BEN: Couple of cans of lager please.

PHOEBE: What's wrong with your wrist?

BEN: Er…I play bass in a band, and it catches on the bridge.

PHOEBE: So you're left handed?

DIANE: Phoebe. Stop it.

PHOEBE: Why do you play in a band?

BEN: 'cause, like, it's a good way of getting your shit out.

PHOEBE: But where does that shit go? Into other people's ears.

DIANE: It must be cold on your narrow boat?

BEN: No, I've got a log burning stove.

PHOEBE: You burn wood?!

BEN: Burning logs is carbon neutral.

PHOEBE: Fantastic! Why don't we burn logs mum!?

DIANE: Good idea, go and chop some.

PHOEBE: We could get some delivered.

BEN: No.

PHOEBE: No, of course not. Oh, it's so difficult isn't it!

BEN: I'm moored at King's Staithe, a lot of driftwood comes down.

PHOEBE: I know King's Staithe. There's about eight narrow boats all painted bright colours with geraniums in a neat row and then on the end there's horrible looking sinister black boat, lying low in the water with old newspapers and towels for curtains. Which one's yours?

BEN: The black one on the end.

(DIANE gives him two lagers. He opens one immediately and swigs.)

BEN: *(To DIANE.)* D'ya get my email?

PHOEBE: She's not been online for two days.

DIANE: Christ was born in a stable, not live on webcam.

BEN: OK. Bust this. We hacked the Hampshire mainframe man! Believe!

KEVIN: Hampshire University?

BEN: I've got the Chinese data.

DIANE: You said "we" hacked?

BEN: My mate Fran, he's the hacker, he's autistic, like Rain Man. He was my best mate in prison.

DIANE: You've been in prison? Why don't I know that?

BEN: Data Protection innit. GBH on my dad.

DIANE: And why was Fran in prison?

BEN: Hacking.

DIANE: Prison's not working is it.

PHOEBE: Was it an open prison?

BEN: No. It was one of those prisons where they, like, lock you up, yeah?

PHOEBE: Did you get anally raped?

BEN: In prison, they rape you, like, spiritually. You wake up, and, like, your Blu-Tack will be gone, yeah? Like, all your Blu-Tack. Just gone, yeah? And the next morning, yeah, it's back again.

KEVIN: What's going on Diane?

DIANE: This is illegal Ben, you've broken the law.

BEN: *(To Kevin.)* It's my term assignment, yeah, to replicate the results of Kieron McKay's Chinese White Pines tree ring study. But he'd refused a Freedom of Information Request which Doctor Cassell made, so I couldn't like, you know, further my education, so I got my mate to hack the mainframe.

KEVIN: Is there any chance of a sandwich?

DIANE: Kevin, I want you to know that at no point did I endorse hacking the Hampshire mainframe. Sausage roll?

KEVIN: Fantastic!

(KEVIN swigs at the red wine. DIANE opens the fridge.)

PHOEBE: Did you learn to talk rap from your parents?

BEN: I'm a comprehensive kid from the city.

PHOEBE: Respect to the mandem.

BEN: Are you taking the piss?

PHOEBE: Are you insecure?

BEN: You freestyle. I'm digging it.

(DIANE has found the sausage rolls.)

DIANE: Warmed up?

KEVIN: Please. Do you remember those sausage rolls we bought in Reykjavic?

DIANE: Don't start Kevin!

(DIANE puts the sausage rolls in either the microwave or the Aga.)

BEN: You know your mum's a brilliant teacher.

PHOEBE: I found her a bit didactic. I didn't go to school. I was home taught.

BEN: But…ain't that…I mean…socially…er…I mean getting taught on your own…er…don't you like kind of miss out on…fuck I dunno, er…

PHOEBE: – social skills?

BEN: Yeah. Where can I boot my lappie?

DIANE: There's power points, here, under the lip, I'll get my laptop.

(DIANE heads to her office, stage left, to get her laptop. BEN stands, and roots around in his pannier for his laptop.)

KEVIN: Is this the tree ring study that they're using to support the Hockey Stick?

BEN: Yeah.

KEVIN: *(To BEN.)* Mmm. Do you believe that we're warmer now than we've ever been?

BEN: Ever been, or in the Holocene?

KEVIN: Christ! You can tell he's one of yours. Of course, in the Holocene. Do you believe we're warmer now than we've ever been in the Holocene?

BEN: I'm a scientist yeah. I can't allow myself to "believe in" anything.

KEVIN: Well good for you. I *believe* we're warmer now than we've ever been, and getting warmer, and the cause of that is us.

(DIANE arrives with her ancient looking laptop and puts it down alongside BEN's.)

PHOEBE: I'm gonna go for a walk, on my own, see if I can get raped.

DIANE: *(To BEN.)* Have you told anyone else about this?

BEN: No. It's me and Fran. We're tight.

(PHOEBE stands.)

PHOEBE: Alright! I'm going to ring Daz, in the pub, he'll sell me some K.

KEVIN: What's K?

DIANE: Ketamine. It's a horse tranquiliser. It's very popular round here.

KEVIN: With horses?

PHOEBE: Wiv the alienated and spiritually moribund rural yoof.

KEVIN: What kind of a trip is it?

PHOEBE: In a K hole you get a separation of mind and body.

KEVIN: Can you get me some?

PHOEBE: Mum! Why is what you're doing now, more important than talking to me?

DIANE: Ben came here, today, because he wanted to show me this data.

PHOEBE: No! This is obviously just an elaborate ruse to see me! Isn't it, Ben?

BEN: Yeah. But let me do this first, alright? Do you want to help? Have you got a laptop?

PHOEBE: I'm twenty-one-years-old. What do you think?

DIANE: That's hers.

BEN: *(To DIANE.)* I've pasted a link in the email I sent you. Can you forward it to Phoebe. I don't know her email.

(PHOEBE moves her laptop and places it down between DIANE's and BEN's thereby separating them with her presence. KEVIN has removed himself from the table and is investigating the sausage roll situation.)

PHOEBE: Are we breaking the law?

KEVIN: Yes!

PHOEBE: Fantastic!

KEVIN: And if anyone asks, I don't care anymore.

DIANE: Your link has taken me to a Slovenian pizza take away site.

BEN: Yeah, it's a dead site. Double click on the Florentina.

PHOEBE: *Fiorentina.* That's the spinachy one with an egg in the middle. Don't you know anything about computing?

KEVIN: I'll have a deep pan meat feast please.

DIANE: It's loading. Slowly.

BEN: How old is that machine?

DIANE: The instruction manual's in Latin.

PHOEBE: Stop it mum! It's embarrassing. She thinks that's funny. What are we doing?

BEN: You know that graph Al Gore has where temperature is steady forever then it, like, suddenly takes off in the twentieth century?

PHOEBE: The hockey stick?

BEN: Yeah.

KEVIN: In that film of his, Al Gore, he's got the y axis upside down.

DIANE: I told you that two years ago.

KEVIN: If you get up really close to the telly, and freeze frame it, you can see. You work your guts out, a lifetime, then some smarmy tit comes along, gets his *y* axis upside down and picks up a Nobel Peace Prize.

DIANE: He's got fat hasn't he, Al Gore.

BEN: Got rich man.

PHOEBE: I like him. For every mouthful of food Al Gore eats he gives two mouthfuls to a starving child in Africa.

DIANE: The poor kid must be huge by now.

PHOEBE: Al Gore cares about the future because his son died.

KEVIN: No! The kid was hit by a car but he didn't die.

PHOEBE: His child didn't die?

DIANE: Have you gone off him now?

PHOEBE: A bit.

BEN: Harsh man! You can't think less of him, 'cause his child *didn't* die.

DIANE: He's also the world's first carbon trading billionaire.

PHOEBE: So he's a carbon trading billionaire, whose child didn't die?

DIANE: Yes.

PHOEBE: What a cunt!

KEVIN: I'll open another bottle.

DIANE: This isn't just Chinese Pines, you've got ten years' of private emails here.

KEVIN: Kieron McKay's private emails?!

DIANE: Merry Christmas Kevin.

(KEVIN looks over their shoulders, whilst opening a bottle.)

PHOEBE: What am I looking for?

BEN: OK, 'cause we've only got the instrument record, that's like thermometers yeah, from about like the nineteenth century, in Paleo we have to kinda like guess, temperatures from what we call proxy data. Proxies are like lake sediments, ice cores, or tree rings.

PHOEBE: I'm the daughter of a climate scientist, I know what a paleoclimate proxy temperature reconstruction is you dick.

DIANE: She only abuses those she loves.

PHOEBE: "The Proxy Lovers". That would be a good name for a band.

KEVIN: I was in a band once. Moscow Jam.

BEN: Cool name.

KEVIN: We were all communists, who liked jam.

BEN: What instrument?

KEVIN: Acoustic and electric guitars.

BEN: Cool. I've brought my guitar. Feel free.

KEVIN: Ta.

PHOEBE: What's the name of your band Ben?

BEN: The Four Horsemen.

PHOEBE: How many are there in the band?

BEN: Seven.

PHOEBE: Have you considered sacking three of them?

DIANE: Why should his band willingly subject itself to the hegemony of language? What kind of rock band is that?

PHOEBE: Because then it'd be a crap band with a congruous name, instead of a crap band with an incongruous name. In anyone's book, that's progress.

BEN: It doesn't matter now anyway.

PHOEBE: Because you've split up?

BEN: Yeah.

PHOEBE: What a waste of thirty seconds that was.

(Kevin has picked up the guitar, taken it out of its case.)

BEN: It's tuned to dropped D.

(KEVIN strums and/or picks half heartedly. And then puts the guitar down.)

KEVIN: I'd better drink a bit more first.

DIANE: Ben, google Chinese White Pines, Phoebe go on Wikipedia and search for Songhua river valley China. I want latitude, climate etc.

KEVIN: Been there. The river freezes every winter, melts every spring, floods the plains, hundreds drown and they all act surprised.

DIANE: Thank you. Professor.

KEVIN: Yeah! They didn't give me an OBE for my apple crumble.

(KEVIN stands and comes over to look over DIANE's shoulder.)

BEN: Chinese White Pines can be susceptible to Cronartium Ribicola.

DIANE: Thanks.

PHOEBE: "The Songhua river valley freezes from November to March".

BEN: Yo!

(High fives with BEN.)

KEVIN: I've still got it. The passion. Yeah.

DIANE: I can't find Kieron McKay's twentieth-century trees.

BEN: I think he's given them, like really obscure labelling.

PHOEBE: *(To BEN.)* Do you want the second of your two beers now Ben?

BEN: I can get it.

PHOEBE: No, you're working.

RICHARD BEAN

(PHOEBE gets his beer.)

DIANE: Forty four trees in the thirteenth-century cohort, OK not many but we can forgive him; hundred and eleven, fourteenth; nearly two hundred, fifteenth; sixty two, sixteenth; four hundred and sixteen, seventeenth; nearly three hundred, eighteenth; eight hundred plus, nineteenth century. Can't find the twentieth-century trees. Looks like he's hidden them. Deliberately.

KEVIN: In case someone hacked the mainframe?

DIANE: I don't know.

KEVIN: Step aside. I'm world class.

PHOEBE: Use mine.

KEVIN: You sure?

PHOEBE: I can share with Ben.

KEVIN: How's he tagged them?

DIANE: C14 is fourteenth century; C15 is fifteenth.

KEVIN: But no C20?

(KEVIN squeezes in taking over PHOEBE's computer.)

BEN: Zero. None. Nandos.

PHOEBE: Do you like Nandos?

BEN: I'm vegetarian.

PHOEBE: I'm anorexic.

BEN: Cool.

PHOEBE: I judge all restaurants by their toilet facilities.

(Finger in throat.)

BEN: I thought that was bulimia.

PHOEBE: Bulimia's gorge purge, I starve purge.

DIANE: Be strong, starve on.

KEVIN: Voila! I've found a cohort of eight trees dated 1952.

86

DIANE: How's he labelled it?

KEVIN: TT52.

DIANE: TT? Christ! It's like cracking a code.

BEN: I got a TT.

PHOEBE: Maybe TT is an acronym for "the trees".

BEN: TT04 is a cohort of five trees alive in 2004.

KEVIN: TT04 is the last of his files.

BEN: That's it man. There's like no more trees.

DIANE: His twentieth century sample is five trees, and eight trees.

KEVIN: n equals thirteen!?

PHOEBE: Is that unlucky?

BEN: It's not statistically significant. n equals thirteen describes the sample size. You knew that, sorry.

PHOEBE: So what's going on then mum?

DIANE: Whatever's going on, it's not science.

KEVIN: Ah! Look! If you right click, you get the individual tree ring graphs.

DIANE: I'm in the 2004 file. Ben do 1952.

BEN: OK! I'm in.

DIANE: What are you getting, any sharp temperature rises?

BEN: The first two trees are flat.

DIANE: I've looked at three trees. Their graphs are flat.

BEN: Flat as road kill.

PHOEBE: That's funny Ben. You can be quite amusing can't you?

BEN: Yeah.

DIANE: There's nothing going on! I'm up to number seven. Flat as a pancake.

PHOEBE: Flat as road kill mum!

DIANE: How the hell do you get a hockey stick from this cohort?!

BEN: I'm one hundred percent road kill.

DIANE: Woah! Look at that! Oh, ho, ho, ho!

(They all look at DIANE's screen.)

KEVIN: What tree is that?

DIANE: Number eight.

PHOEBE: – sexy Kate!

DIANE: – is she late!

PHOEBE: – Harry Tate!

BEN: Bingo rhymes freestyle, man, I dig!

PHOEBE: Bingo is cutting edge in the countryside.

KEVIN: A perfect hockey stick.

BEN: One tree.

DIANE: Do you see, Phoebe? After 1950, this tree, just takes off.

PHOEBE: Why?

BEN: Kieron McKay would say it's temperature rise.

KEVIN: Mmm.

PHOEBE: Yeah, I think he's right.

DIANE: I think Sexy Kate is a young tree in 1890 surrounded by mature trees, struggling for water, growing in the shade, in 1950 there's a storm, the old trees fall down, because they're weakened by –

BEN: – Cronartium Ribicola –

DIANE: – the dead trees fertilise the ground, and sexy Kate feels the sun for the first time, and has her fifteen minutes of fame.

PHOEBE: But why did they cut our lovely sexy Kate down?

BEN: I guess they needed the wood.

DIANE: I cannot believe it. One tree!

KEVIN: That's it, the end of the file!

(BEN stands, moves away from the laptops. Picks up his guitar.)

DIANE: One bloody tree. One tree!

BEN: That is like the single most significant tree in the world man.

PHOEBE: Your tree in the Maldives is one tree.

KEVIN: Yes, ha ha! Yes! Good point.

BEN: Is this dangerous? Like globally, economically. If I post this on the net, I mean.

KEVIN: The carbon markets are not going to respond to one bit of bodged science coming out of Hampshire.

BEN: But the world economy is already dodgy dodgy.

PHOEBE: I like it when you say words twice.

BEN: Yeah?

PHOEBE: Yeah.

DIANE: I can imagine carbon trading collapsing.

KEVIN: Because of this!?

PHOEBE: Banks close their doors, seal up their ATMs. Riots. Street fighting.

BEN: Anarchy in the UK.

PHOEBE: Chavs drive into the countryside and pull crops up with their bare hands, and discover the dignity of labour.

BEN: Farmers fire at the urban working class from motorway bridges.

PHOEBE: Babylon is burning, ruined, wrecked.

BEN: Disease, war, and famine.

PHOEBE: No one can survive. Except one man. Mum?

DIANE: Mel Gibson. Mel is an astronaut returning from Venus with gas.

PHOEBE: Mel Gibson is the last man standing. Humanity is on the brink of extinction. Ben?

BEN: Mel can't find a woman but befriends a wolf called Dennis.

PHOEBE: Dennis and Mel spend twenty years wandering about in a cinematic mist looking for a human female. Mum?

DIANE: One day Mel sees a beautiful girl –

PHOEBE: – a beautiful nude girl bathing naked in a river, with no clothes on. Who would that be Ben?

BEN: Er…Gemma Arterton.

PHOEBE: I am so disappointed. Mel and Gemma must make a baby, but, plot twist, Mel's character is gay.

DIANE: But fortunately, Gemma understands the principles of aversion therapy so she draws pictures of boys in the sand, gets Mel to look at them whilst she thrashes him with a stick until he becomes heterosexual.

PHOEBE: Brilliant! Mel and Gemma make love!

(PHOEBE kisses BEN. It's a proper kiss. Outside it is now dark.)

KEVIN: Bloody hell.

DIANE: Christ! I've seen hard-core porn that was easier to watch.

PHOEBE: Would you like to walk around a Medieval plague village in the dark, with me, Ben? Now? Please.

BEN: Yes, but my shoes are wet.

PHOEBE: You can borrow some wellies.

DIANE: It's too late for Wharram Percy. It's dark, and the snow is drifting.

KEVIN: What is this Wharram Percy? A kind of lost village?

DIANE: How does one lose a village?

PHOEBE: The black death wiped them out.

DIANE: Can you explain something to me Kevin? Every year Phoebe and I walk around Wharram Percy. *Every year* I explain to her that the residents left the village in the sixteenth century because there was a change of land use. The landlord wanted to graze sheep, which meant an end to arable farming, so everyone packed their bags and left to look for work elsewhere.

KEVIN: How prosaic.

DIANE: Yes. But this generation –

PHOEBE: – it's not my generation that has fucked the planet.

DIANE: This generation, are disaster junkies. Armageddon in three acts.

PHOEBE: Fuck off.

DIANE: It's as if their every last twitching synapse has been transplanted from the stolen corpse of a Hollywood screen writer. Why be content with "a change of land use" when you can have the drama of "wiped out by the Black Death". Every day they wake up craving a narrative fix. When they see a photograph of a polar bear, hitching a lift on a passing ice flow, they cannot see a wild animal at ease in its natural habitat. What they see is the last five minutes of Titanic! That one ton carnivor's contented yawn becomes Leonardo DiCaprio's hopeless scream as he drifts inexorably away from that posh girl who's normally in a corset.

BEN: Kate Winslet.

PHOEBE: Gemma Arterton and Kate Winslet?

DIANE: If you point out that Armageddon has been prophesied a thousand times, and has always turned out to be wrong, they do that face which they keep in reserve for the moment in a restaurant when you order veal.

(KEVIN is clicking on the computer now.)

KEVIN: This is a text file right?

BEN: Yeah.

KEVIN: I want to see what McKay told Toby at Nature about n equals thirteen.

PHOEBE: So, are you a sceptic now Professor?

KEVIN: This is not the road to Damascus. This is one scientist bodging. We've all done it. I know the planet's warming from the ice cores I've drilled myself. I go to Greenland every year. Actually, D –

DIANE: – don't call me D!

KEVIN: You should come to Greenland with me. You can stand on the glaciers and watch them melting.

DIANE: I'm not going anywhere cold with you. I know how you keep your hands warm.

PHOEBE: You're excited though aren't you, you've stopped drinking.

DIANE: He can see a way of bringing down Hampshire University.

KEVIN: Correct.

BEN: Would it be alright, if I like played a song?

DIANE: Sure.

BEN: I wrote this song for you.

PHOEBE/DIANE: Me? / For me?

BEN: Whatever.

PHOEBE: Give me a drink.

(DIANE pours PHOEBE a glass of wine, and herself.)

DIANE: I'll put some pizzas in. Pizzas!?

KEVIN/BEN: Yeah / Great.

PHOEBE: This is going to be really weird. I mean…shouldn't this be in private?

(During the next DIANE gets pizzas from the fridge. BEN sings and plays.)

BEN: *(Adagio.)*
I met her first in the fall
she looked past me at the wall

(KEVIN and DIANE share a quizzical glance, as if to say "oh dear".)

my lobster skin and lobster hair
were not what she had in mind
at all

met her once again in town
we're both a week older now
and I felt like an ocean inside
but spoke to her confidently
do you remember me?

(Spoken.) She said – no, I don't, go away.

(They laugh.)

BEN: *(Allegro.)*
but it's early days,
and things might change
and love might wax
and love might wane
and the sun might shine
and the rain might rain
on us some time one day

(Adagio.)
in the spring I saw her again
through the window of a train
and destiny took the controls
and waved my arms joyously
I'm here, hello, yes it's me!

(Spoken.) nothing

(Allegro.)
but it's early days,
and things might change
and love might wax
and love might wane
and the sun might shine
and the rain might rain
on us some time one day

(KEVIN and DIANE applaud and cheer. PHOEBE has her hand over her mouth.)

KEVIN/DIANE: Brilliant mate. / It's lovely!

BEN: *(To PHOEBE.)* Did you like it?

PHOEBE: Some bits were alright. *(To BEN.)* Do you like badgers?

DIANE: No, you're not going outside! It's dark now.

PHOEBE: It's dark!? I'm not a child! Ben, do you like badgers?

BEN: Badgers? Dunno. I haven't like properly thought it through.

(PHOEBE puts her coat and hat on and picks up a bottle of wine.)

PHOEBE: I'm going to go and sit in the observatory oblique stroke badger hide.

DIANE: *(To BEN.)* We have a shed, with a telescope. You can watch the stars or you can watch the badgers.

PHOEBE: Shagging.

KEVIN: You won't see any badgers shagging in winter.

DIANE: In winter, "badger watching" means drinking, and smoking dope.

KEVIN: *(To PHOEBE.)* Oh right, you keep your stash in the hide do you?

PHOEBE: No.

KEVIN: I could do with a joint. I've had a difficult last ten years.

PHOEBE: Maybe, but I don't like you.

DIANE: Offer her money.

KEVIN: I'll give you some money.

PHOEBE: Do I look like a dealer?

DIANE: We need to find Ben a coat. Will this be a problem? It's mine?

BEN: Cool.

(He puts the coat on. BEN slips the woolly hat on and pulls it down.)

PHOEBE: Oh God, I can't watch, it's so Freudian.

DIANE: Get out!

KEVIN: Here.

(He manages to give PHOEBE a fiver, which she takes. They exit.)

DIANE: Ben will have to stay the night. What about you?

KEVIN: I'll be no trouble.

DIANE: If you try anything, I'll stick this…I'll stick a bread knife through your kidneys.

KEVIN: But you wouldn't do that really.

DIANE: I would if I could find one.

(She is puzzled. Looks in drawers etc.)

KEVIN: Kieron McKay's got a spare ticket for a Rolling Stones gig at Wembley Stadium. He wants forty quid for it. Cheapskate.

DIANE: What year is that?

KEVIN: 1999.

DIANE: I only let you in today Kevin because I'm frightened.

(She goes to her office and comes back with a Christmas card, in an envelope.)

I got a Christmas card. There's no stamp. They know where I live.

(She hands it to him. He reads it.)

KEVIN: "Continue your column in the Torygraph and you will get a visit from Father Christmas. The Sacred Earth Militia."

DIANE: And two weeks ago I opened the barn to find that the Jag had a flat. I found a screw in the tyre.

KEVIN: You drove over some screws.

DIANE: The screw was drilled into the wall of the tyre. The wall!

KEVIN: Was there any evidence of a break in?

DIANE: None. The barn was bolted and the padlock locked.

KEVIN: Do you keep the keys, you know, lying about, on a hook, in here?

DIANE: No. On my key ring.

(She shows the key ring.)

KEVIN: Have you told the police?

DIANE: Yes. They wanted to come and look at security. I said no. This is the kind of thing that can flip Phoebe. I can feel them, watching me.

KEVIN: You're being paranoid.

DIANE: I'm being rational!

KEVIN: Is the front door locked?

DIANE: And bolted, it's never used.

KEVIN: Bolt that door too. The kids'll have to knock.

DIANE: Do you think they're OK in the hide?

KEVIN: What would The Sacred Earth Militia do with the
kids? Kill them? My sister, London, drives a big fuck off
4x4, she gets mad green stickers on her windscreen all the
time. But there's this grungy converted ambulance camper
van, ancient, three litre diesel, filthy –

DIANE: – never gets a sticker.

KEVIN: Never. What's that about?

DIANE: Green is a proxy for anything. Class war. Hate your
dad. Hate America. All religions are shot through with
inconsistencies.

KEVIN: It's not a religion!

DIANE: It's the perfect religion for the narcissistic age. It
provides a clear definition of sin. Drive to work – sinful.
Cycle – righteous. Fly to Crete – sinful. Go camping in the
New Forest – righteous.

KEVIN: In the rain.

DIANE: Martyrdom. Why drink the blood of Christ, when
you can score a regular epiphany recycling The London
Review of Books.

KEVIN: You just like driving Jaguars!

DIANE: Cars are liberating, democratic, and feminist. And the
day when Greenpeace has succeeded in pricing the poor
out of the skies and off the roads will not be a good day for
the planet, it will be a good day for totalitarianism.

KEVIN: What do these buggers want? To go back to nature?

DIANE: Nature is hell. Nature is hunger, cold, dying in childbirth. I want electricity, a car, central heating, and I don't want to have to eat my own pigs, I want to eat someone else's pigs.

KEVIN: You could eat my pigs D?

DIANE: Stop trying to get in my knickers!

KEVIN: God put me on earth to try and get into your knickers.

DIANE: You're an atheist.

KEVIN: I am, yes, but He isn't. What do you make of this? "I've binned the tree ring data, and pasted in the instrument record from 1960 to bury the downturn. If it's good enough for MBH, it's good enough for me."

DIANE: MBH is Mann, Bradley, Hughes.

KEVIN: The Hockey Stick team.

DIANE: Yup.

KEVIN: Do these tree ring guys make a habit of pasting in the instrument record on the end of a proxy series?

DIANE: You're not seriously telling me that you did not know that *Professor*?

KEVIN: No! Fucking no! They can't do that! That's like a vegetarian getting his blood sugar up with a bacon sandwich. Why don't I know this!?

DIANE: I knew that.

KEVIN: Yes, but you're a fucking clever cloggs.

DIANE: I'm more interested in "bury the downturn". He's hiding stuff again! What's the downturn Kev?

KEVIN: The downturn in temperatures. Obviously.

DIANE: The last ten years?

KEVIN: Yeah. We've had ten, eleven years of downturn, no temperature increase, and enough cold winters to bolster the sceptic argument.

DIANE: No. If he was trying to bury the last decade's downturn in temperatures, he wouldn't paste in the instrument record. That would show the downturn. What's the date of this email?

KEVIN: 1999.

DIANE: Before the downturn in temperatures.

KEVIN: Ah, yes.

DIANE: Do a text search on "downturn".

(KEVIN does that.)

DIANE: Woah! Busy!

KEVIN: "I can't get a signal with this data. There's a downturn across the board since 1965."

DIANE: Next.

KEVIN: "I'm banging my head against the downturn. Temperatures are going up, and the trees aren't interested." Does that mean what I think it means?

DIANE: The downturn is the collapse of the correlation between temperatures and tree rings.

KEVIN: This is a tree ring guy, admitting that trees are lousy thermometers!

DIANE: After 1965.

KEVIN: D, if trees are lousy thermometers now, they've always been lousy thermometers.

DIANE: Look, at this one. They're speculating on why trees have stopped responding. Carbon dioxide fertilisation, drought, pollution.

KEVIN: Yes! I've been saying tree rings are lousy proxies for years.

DIANE: You've got exactly what you want. Hampshire University is all tree rings.

KEVIN: Haha! Catalan won't want to hang their jacket on a shaky nail! This is brilliant news for us Diane!

DIANE: Us? There is no us Kevin. You sacked me because I'm mad.

KEVIN: You're mad, I'm mad. Who cares! Today, looking at the sea, I thought of King Cnut, and his – what's that word, sounds like you should eat it with pitta bread and olives?

DIANE: Hubris.

KEVIN: Hubris. Yes. Are we all Cnuts? Am I a Cnut?

DIANE: How are you spelling it?

KEVIN: C.N.U.T.

DIANE: In that order?

KEVIN: Yeah.

DIANE: Cnut was a canny operator. In 1020 they were growing corn in Greenland, and if it's warm enough for corn it's too warm for ice. Sea level rise must've been a problem, and as King of Denmark and England Cnut would have been a one man IPCC getting grief from landowners seeing their acres slipping under water. Knowing he was powerless he set up a photo op, a media stunt, to demonstrate his impotence in the face of nature.

KEVIN: I didn't know that.

DIANE: You didn't know that, because Cnut commanding the tide is a better story.

KEVIN: You're such a good teacher. I'd like you to come back to work with me.

DIANE: Fuck off!

KEVIN: And swear at me.

(DIANE throws something at him.)

And throw things at me.

DIANE: You're offering me my job back?

KEVIN: Yes. That is what I'm doing right now.

DIANE: Because the argument is the science?

KEVIN: Exactly.

DIANE: And you'll need me if you win the Catalan contract when this gets out about McKay.

KEVIN: We'll be busy, yes.

DIANE: You can't go public with this. Hacking is a criminal offence.

KEVIN: What can we do?

DIANE: Wikileaks.

KEVIN: Where are the ethics in all this?

DIANE: In the blender.

(Banging on the door. The door is bolted. DIANE jumps, frightened.)

PHOEBE: *(Off.)* Mum!

KEVIN: Come back and teach D. Please.

(DIANE opens the door, lets her in.)

PHOEBE: Why have you bolted the door?

DIANE: What is it?

PHOEBE: Ben said I can live with him on his barge! I want to move out tomorrow. Is that alright?

DIANE: Has he got a license?

PHOEBE: You don't need a license to live with a woman.

KEVIN: No, you need a training course.

DIANE: I want to see the boat first.

PHOEBE: What do you need to know? It's black.

DIANE: I want to know that it's safe.

PHOEBE: Fascist.

DIANE: I'm your mother! This is a reasonable request.

(She gets the pizzas out of the oven.)

Tell Ben to come in for his pizza.

PHOEBE: Ben doesn't want to eat.

DIANE: Oh!

PHOEBE: But I'm...I might have a bit.

KEVIN: B b b b b b –

DIANE: – shutup Kevin.

PHOEBE: Why is he doing an impression of Billy from from One Flew Over the Cuckoo's Nest?

KEVIN: I wasn't. Honestly.

DIANE: OK, tell Ben I want to talk to him.

PHOEBE: About what?

DIANE: About the joys of living with a purging anorexic. And close that door!

PHOEBE: Don't you dare fuck this up for me.

(PHOEBE turns to go. She looks at KEVIN.)

PHOEBE: What are you looking at?

KEVIN: I was hoping for a joint.

PHOEBE: I don't deliver. I'm not Ocado.

(She turns and is gone. Door closed. KEVIN stands, intent on going out to the hide to get a joint.)

KEVIN: Can I smoke in here? I think they want to be alone.

DIANE: I don't fucking care any more.

KEVIN: I lived on a wreck of a boat once and – (it didn't have)

DIANE: – get out!

(KEVIN leaves. The door is closed. DIANE, stressed, tries to compose herself. Looks for a knife. The knife block is empty. She checks the drawers, the sink. She is confused, now scared, as she thinks about it. She looks around the room, opens the walk in cupboard, looks in,

*closes it. She stands with both hands rooted on the table, she looks
down, breathes. Her mobile phone rings.)*

DIANE: *(On the phone, speaking loudly.)* Youssef! …yes, I can
hear you, can you hear me?…yes, Phoebe is here and
we're having a lovely Christmas… there's a lot of snow…
what?…OK…a group of environmentalists?

(She sits. Enter BEN. He listens.)

…were they Maldivian?…can you email photographs…
thank you Youssef…yes, this must be costing you an arm
and a leg… of course…let's do this by email. Thanks
Youssef…Yes, I'll be back in the summer. Goodbye.

(Off the phone.) Some "group of environmentalists" has dug
up my tree.

BEN: They dug a tree up? Environmentalists? We're out of
paraffin.

DIANE: On the floor. In here.

*(She opens the cupboard. BEN goes in and comes out with the
paraffin.)*

Phoebe is a bully. And it's not a rational decision to choose
to live with an anorexic.

BEN: I don't want it to be a rational decision.

DIANE: It's not a silly thing about not eating much. If she has
a bad couple of months, she might die. She came close last
year.

BEN: What, she nearly, like, actually died?

DIANE: Every organ in the body needs fuel in order to
function. And I would rather have her alive than everyone
in Bangladesh, or Tuvalu, or Suffolk. And every glacier
in the world, and every coral reef, and every single last
bloody polar bear can die, drown, melt, go impossibly
acidic and fall to pieces and I honestly wouldn't care, as
long as I've still got her. If you're not serious about living
with her –

BEN: – living on the boat wasn't my idea you know.

DIANE: She's twenty one. She should've left home, me, years ago.

BEN: Has she never lived away from home then?

DIANE: We tried university. She was seventeen. It was my fault. She stayed a week. She was appalled at the lack of intellectual rigour of the lecturers.

BEN: Which university?

DIANE: Oxford.

BEN: I just think she's slammin', and I was going to ask her out.

DIANE: Listen! I think she may have started menstruating again. Can you try very hard please, not to get her pregnant.

BEN: I guess with her not eating, getting pregnant could be –

DIANE: – no, no, she has threatened to kill herself. Bringing children into the world is irresponsible, apparently. Do you need condoms?

BEN: I've got enough for today.

DIANE: Get some more.

(She gives him a twenty pound note, thinks, then gives him another.)

And she might threaten to go to church. Let her. Don't argue. Right! Food, I know we don't talk about it, but calories, minimum 800 –

(PHOEBE appears at the door. Top half open.)

PHOEBE: Trapped in a country house with two girls. Is that a favourite masturbation fantasy Ben?

BEN: Not especially.

PHOEBE: What are you talking about?

BEN: Pizza toppings.

PHOEBE: She's a control freak you know. You think she's being open, and generous, and giving but she's really only drawing you in and when you're not looking she ties strings around your arms and legs and neck. Strings she can pull. In the future.

BEN: I'll get the stove working.

(BEN picks up the paraffin and is gone. Door closed. PHOEBE bolts it from the inside.)

PHOEBE: I don't need my mother to pimp for me. OK?

DIANE: I prefer the word facilitation.

PHOEBE: And stop trying to change him. That first time, in your office, he was beautiful, spiritual, and heroic.

DIANE: We all love a martyr.

PHOEBE: I fell in love with him that day.

DIANE: You fell in love with the idea of him.

PHOEBE: It's a start!

DIANE: Go and stare at the fucking stars, go on, you're a young person, go and be overwhelmed by your own insignificance!

PHOEBE: I will because there are phenomena in this universe that can't be pushed around a petri dish. You have to have faith. You know, I think your scepticism is nothing more than a catastrophic failure of the imagination.

DIANE: He doesn't believe.

PHOEBE: Stop trying to make him like you. I'm asking for a contract.

DIANE: Maeve will only let us contract achievable behaviour change.

PHOEBE: Don't you dare destroy him. Stop teaching him! Stop evangelising your lousy religion!

DIANE: He chose a science course!

PHOEBE: Empiricism is a fucking ism like any other fucking ism.

(PHOEBE punches DIANE.)

DIANE: No! Phoebe, please! Don't start that!

(PHOEBE picks up a bottle, and attacks DIANE. DIANE protects herself by curling up and covering her face with her arms and hands. She's done this many times before. PHOEBE lays in to her.)

DIANE: Phoebe, you'll hurt me!

PHOEBE: Stop teaching him crap!

(Another blow.)

DIANE: Agh! Stop it!

(PHOEBE lays in with punches as well as the bottle.)

PHOEBE: I don't want you fucking with his head. I don't want him to change! Stop it! Stop teaching, teaching, fucking teaching!

DIANE: Agh! You're hurting me Phoebe!

(PHOEBE is breathing hard. She takes her time. Silence.)

PHOEBE: Mum! I've got that pain, across my shoulders.

DIANE: You've got yourself excited. Just slow down.

(PHOEBE puts the bottle down.)

Sit down. Breathe.

PHOEBE: My shoulders mum! Agh! My shoulders! Aggggh!

DIANE: Just keep breathing, I'm getting your nitro.

PHOEBE: Oh my God! Ohhh!

(KEVIN tries the door. It's locked. He knocks. Then looks through the window. DIANE lets him in, and goes for her phone. KEVIN enters, joint in hand.)

KEVIN: If we'd had skunk when we were kids, really, we wouldn't have got a lot done. What this party needs is some Lynyrd Skynrd.

PHOEBE: Agggghhh! Mum!

KEVIN: What's this now?

DIANE: We're trying to stay calm.

KEVIN: Why?

DIANE: We are both working hard to ward off a heart attack.

KEVIN: A heart attack! Bloody hell, what do you want me to do?

DIANE: *(To KEVIN.)* Get the first aid kit down. There!

(On the phone.) Hello. Ambulance please, thank you. …my daughter is having a heart attack…she's 21, she's anorexic…I'm sorry you will have to trust me I have seen these symptoms twice in the last year…

(KEVIN finds the first aid kit. DIANE takes it off him.)

I'm about to give her three shots of sublingual nitrostat… yes! I've done it before…yes, we are prepared, yes, but I am not a medic, we still need an ambulance please! …a helicopter will be fine.

(DIANE takes the first aid box and gives the phone to KEVIN.)

Tell them the address. They can land near the pond.

(During the next DIANE administers the nitrostat to PHOEBE and KEVIN takes the phone.)

PHOEBE: Agggh! Mum!

DIANE: Just breathe baby, don't do anything else.

KEVIN: Hello…yes, you can land next to the pond, the address here is…

(DIANE points to some bills on the wall. KEVIN reads them.)

Manor Barns...Fimber...post code YO25 5BG. OK... Is there anyone here with paramedic training? ...no...is there anyone here who has carried out what? ...say it again?

DIANE: Cardiopulmonory Resucitation. No!

(DIANE shakes her head.)

KEVIN: Yeah?...er, no...

DIANE: Fuck! This is the real thing.

KEVIN: The helicopter is on it's way...do we have a defibrilator?

DIANE: No.

KEVIN: No...Can you talk me through CPR?...No, OK...yes, she has had the nitrosat...good, that's handy, the helicopter was in the sky already.

DIANE: Come on Phoebs! Don't do this to me! You can't do this! I'm not gonna let you get away with this! Breathe! One more spray!

(PHOEBE is not responding.)

She's not breathing. Come on girl! I want you to breathe baby! For Christ's sake, breathe! Breathe girl! Breathe!

(There is the sound thump on the floorboards above. KEVIN instinctively looks upwards. There are heavy footsteps towards the stairs.)

KEVIN: Jesus! What the fuck is that! Is Ben upstairs?

DIANE: Someone's in the house! I told you. Come on Phoebe! Kevin! NO! She's stopped breathing.

KEVIN: Oh Christ.

(GEOFF appears quickly, arms raised as if to say "don't worry I can explain".)

KEVIN: Geoff?! What –

GEOFF: – I can explain.

DIANE: He's Sacred Earth Militia.

GEOFF: Maybe, but I was 42 Commando. In the Falklands. I was our section medic.

DIANE: You can do CPR?

GEOFF: Yeah.

DIANE: Do it then. She's had three shots of nitrosat.

GEOFF: Sublingual.

DIANE: You know?

GEOFF: You can hear every word upstairs.

DIANE: How long have you been up there?

GEOFF: Since this morning. We were gonna kidnap you. The others'll be here soon. I know what I'm doing alright, but CPR ain't like on the telly, I don't want you getting your hopes up. It's a last resort, so it's not exactly got the statistics behind it. But I was 42 Commando, so give me a chance.

(GEOFF approaches PHOEBE and physically throws an obstacle out of his way so that can sit with one knee by PHOEBE's head and one knee by her chest. He does a skilful head tilt chin lift.

GEOFF: *(The following he says for no one's benefit but his own.)* Head tilt, chin lift. Look, listen, feel.

(GEOFF bends his head down to PHOEBE's to listen for breathing. He looks for breathing, ie: a rising and falling chest. And he feels for air. He doesn't find any evidence of breathing. GEOFF places his mouth on PHOEBE's and administers two short breaths, looking for evidence of a rising chest. He then checks for a pulse with two fingers, not the thumb, on the carotid artery [neck].)

One, two, three, four, five, six, seven, eight, nine, ten.

(GEOFF does not find a pulse and so begins CPR. He gets in position and counts as he does 30 compressions in 23 seconds.)

One, two, three, four, five, six, seven, eight, nine, ten,
come on love! You can do it! eleven, twelve, thirteen
– *(Continuing during next up to 23.)*

(Enter BEN as GEOFF continues. He closes the door behind him.)

BEN: There's like guys piling out of a van in the road. Who's
he? What's happened?

GEOFF: Lock your door! Twenty, twenty one, twenty two, and
twenty three.

(On 23 GEOFF delivers two in breaths to PHOEBE.)

KEVIN: They're Sacred Earth Militia.

*(KEVIN bolts the door. We now see The Sacred Earth Militia
approach. Three of them in ski masks and fatigues and black woolly
hats. They have torches which they shine in through the windows.
They try the door. GEOFF has started a second course of CPR,
counting as he goes.)*

GEOFF: Scare 'em. Get violent with 'em. Go on. There's onny
me what don't mind a fight, and right now, I'm busy.

*(There is banging on the door. BEN goes into the cupboard, comes out
with a pitch fork, and rushes to the door. He opens the top half of the
stable door revealing one member of the Militia standing there. BEN
lunges at him/her with the pitch fork. He/she screams.)*

BEN: All hippies must die! I'm gonna rip your fucking head off
and shit down your neck!

*(The Militia girl backs off. BEN is now out in the garden, we can
see him strutting around the garden brandishing the pitch fork. The
Sacred Earth Militia retreat.)*

GEOFF: Twenty two, twenty three.

*(GEOFF administers two more breaths. Checks for a pulse. Continues
CPR.)*

BEN: Do you want some! Come on, come on, come on. Eh,
eh, eh, eh. Come on then!

(As the sound of the helicopter kicks in, very loud as it gets low to land, lights beam across the stage, BEN and KEVIN are both lit in the garden armed, mad, screaming, both armed with weapons, both screaming at the Militia-like demons, GEOFF is steady and continuing CPR.)

DIANE: No?

GEOFF: I'm sorry. One, two, three etc

DIANE: Don't be sorry Geoff. Come on Phoebs! You can do it!

(As the sound intensifies from the helicopter landing, the lights fade. Music for the scene change. Maybe a band version of BEN's song, though properly doom laden at first.)

End of Act Four.

Act Five

SCENE ONE

(August the same year. Afternoon. Sunshine, bird song. The door is open. A car arrives, engine off, doors open, doors closed. Enter KEVIN, dressed in a black suit, white shirt, and black tie. He could be dressed for a funeral. The door is open, with summer sun streaming on to the kitchen floor. KEVIN pushes the door, and walks in without knocking. He looks around. He sits. He looks at his watch. At one point he puts his head in his hands, as if stressed, tense. Enter DIANE. She is wearing a summer frock, and wedding hat. She looks bright and happy.)

KEVIN: You look gorgeous D.

DIANE: Thank you. You look dressed for a funeral.

KEVIN: You said you would have a button hole for me.

DIANE: I do. I'm talking about the tie. It's terrible.

(They kiss, it's a welcoming kiss. DIANE pins a wedding button hole flower on his jacket.)

KEVIN: My father said never trust a man in a tie.

DIANE: Take it off then.

(KEVIN takes the tie off.)

KEVIN: Thanks.

(Enter PHOEBE via the stairs door. PHOEBE is about eight months pregnant and wearing a full white wedding dress.)

KEVIN: You look fantastic.

PHOEBE: Thank you Professor Kevin. You look like shit.

KEVIN: *(To DIANE.)* Is shit good?

DIANE: No.

PHOEBE: Mum's in a mood.

KEVIN: Is she? Why?

DIANE: She wouldn't let me invite my mother.

PHOEBE: Every girl has the right not to have the BNP at her wedding. Anyway, she wouldn't have come even if she had been invited.

DIANE: She would. It's a white wedding.

(Enter BEN from upstairs. He's dressed in a black kilt, with black socks, black Doc Martens and a black tuxedo. It's all charity shop but he looks fantastic.)

BEN: Alright! I'm nervous.

KEVIN: I didn't know you were Scottish.

BEN: I'm not. This is all Help the Aged had left.

DIANE: You know it's unlucky for a groom to see the wedding dress before the church?

PHOEBE: Is it unlucky for the bride to have sex on the morning of her wedding?

DIANE: Yes, if it's with someone other than the groom.

PHOEBE: *(To BEN.)* Have you written a speech lover?

BEN: I've written a new song.

PHOEBE: *(To DIANE.)* Oh isn't he beautiful mum. My intended.

DIANE: Yes, I chose well.

PHOEBE: Bitch.

KEVIN: Right! It's me and the bride in the Jag, with the top down. You're driving the Prius, and Ben is on his bike. Shall I take the guitar for you?

BEN: Na, I'm cool. I better set off now. See you down there.

(BEN kisses PHOEBE.)

DIANE: That's also unlucky.

(BEN leaves. PHOEBE follows him out.)

KEVIN: Are you ready?

DIANE: No. I'll never be ready.

(DIANE shuffles some notes on the table.)

KEVIN: What's this? Your speech.

DIANE: Yes. I'm worried it might be a bit pompous.

KEVIN: Would you like me to peer review it?

DIANE: Please.

(KEVIN shuts the door.)

KEVIN: Go on then!

DIANE: Friends. What a beautiful day. What a really very beautiful day. Wharram Percy is my favourite place. Phoebe and I come here every Boxing Day. We walk around this abandoned village and we try and imagine life in Medieval times. No electricity, no central heating, no cars, sharing the house with a cow. That's easier.

KEVIN: *(Laughs.)* No, no. You don't need to say "that's easier".

DIANE: Thank you Kevin. You're a kind man.

KEVIN: It's not kindness Diane. I'm fucking nuts about you.

DIANE: This year has not been easy. It has been *my* annus horribilis.

KEVIN: No. Don't say that. People start thinking about horrible arses.

DIANE: Do they?

KEVIN: I think normal people do, yes. Nobody had the guts to tell the Queen.

DIANE: This last year has not been easy. Pause. Ironic laughter. In the middle of my personal hell something happened. Ben and Phoebe fell in love. They fell in love as many young people do gazing at the stars in wonder whilst out of their heads on skunk. But this year, I've changed my opinion of the stars, I've decided that the stars are rubbish.

KEVIN: Oh!? I like it!

DIANE: The stars are dead, burning rocks. Barren, lifeless. Stars don't consider your feelings, they never write, they never phone, they forget your birthday. The stars know nothing of love. Stars are self obsessed, look at me, look at me, look at me. Stars are thick. Which star came up with the idea of using the energy stored in a lump of fossilized swamp to power the internet? Which star invented air travel, the internal combustion engine? Which star split the atom? The stars are God's mistakes. We are the miracle. Life. Human intelligence. Human innovation, creativity, invention. That is why every night the stars gaze down on us in awe.

(She is crying.)

It's too pompous for a wedding isn't it?

KEVIN: Yes. But it's true, and it's beautiful.

DIANE: And it's all about me, again. It's always about me!

KEVIN: Yes. It's all about you.

(He comforts her. They hold each other. They don't kiss.)

DIANE: I never cry. Never.

(She exits, he follows.)

Fade to black.

The End.